DAY TRADING FOR

BEGINNERS 2022

Everything you need to know to start

day trading with profits in 2022

Christian Hum

Copyright Christian Hum © 2022,

All rights reserved.

Table of Content

Introduction 4

Chapter 1: Fundamental Trading Strategies 27

Chapter 2: Trading like a Hedge 58

Chapter 3: Best times to trade for Individual 80

Chapter 4: What moves the Market 94

Conclusion 166

Introduction

There was a time years ago when the only people who could actively trade in the stock market were those who worked for large financial institutions, brokers, and trading houses. However, over the past 25 years, developments such as the growth of consumer discounts and online trading, coupled with the rapid distribution of news in the world and the lowest commissions, have limited the play — or should we say trade — platform. In recent years, the popularity of trading platforms such as Robinhood and 0% commissions has made it easier for retail investors to trade like experts.

Day trading can be a very lucrative business (as long as you do it right). But it can also be a slight challenge for beginners, especially those who are not fully prepared with a well-planned strategy. Even experienced day traders can earn a living and lose.

So, what exactly is day trading, and how does it work?

Important Things

Day traders are active traders who make day-to-day strategies to make a profit from changing the price of a particular commodity.

Everyday trading uses a variety of strategies and strategies to achieve perceived market inefficiencies.

Day trading is often characterized by technical analysis and requires a high level of self-discipline and intelligence.

What is Day Trading?

Fundamentals of Day Trading

Day trading usually refers to the practice of buying and selling securities within a single day of trading. It can occur in any marketplace but is most common in foreign exchange (forex) and stock markets. Day traders are usually well educated and well-funded. They use high performance and short-term trading strategies to make money through the small price movements that occur in the most liquid stocks or in stocks.

Day traders are accustomed to events that create a temporary market movement. News-based trading is a popular method. Scheduled declarations such as economic statistics, corporate earnings, or interest rates are below market expectations and market intelligence performance. Markets respond when expectations are not met or exceeded — often sudden, dramatic movements — which can greatly benefit day traders.

Day traders use many intraday strategies. These strategies include:

Scalping: This strategy tries to make a small profit by changing small amounts throughout the day.

Globalization: This strategy primarily uses support and resistance levels to determine buy and sell decisions.

Media-based marketing: This strategy often takes advantage of trading opportunities from high volatility in media events.

High-frequency trading (HFT): These techniques use sophisticated algorithms to exploit the inefficiency of small or temporary markets.

Controversial Practice

Profitability for day trading is a topic that is often discussed on Wall Street. Day trading scams have enticed beginners by promising huge profits in a short period of time. Unfortunately, the notion that this type of trading is a form of a get-rich-quick scheme persists. Some people trade during the day without knowing enough. But there are traders of the day who make a living successfully despite — or perhaps because of — the risks.

Many professional financial executives and financial advisers avoid trading day in and day out. They argue that, in most cases, the reward does not justify the risk. On the contrary, those who trade during the day insist on having a profit. Day trading for profit is possible, but the success rate is naturally low because it is risky in nature and requires great skill. In addition, economists and financial professionals alike argue that, over time, effective trading strategies often undermine the basic indicator of inactivity, especially after investments and taxes are considered.

Day trading is not for everyone and involves significant risks. In addition, it requires a deep understanding of how markets work and the various strategies for making a profit in the short term. While the success stories of the wealthy as a day trader often get a lot of media attention, remember that this is not the case for most everyday traders: Many will go out, and many will simply stay afloat. In addition, do not underestimate the role of luck and good time — although skill is a key factor. Unfortunately, even the most experienced trader of the day can be overwhelmed.

Day Trader Features

Professional day traders — those who trade for a living instead of hobbies — usually do well in this field.[2] They usually have in-depth knowledge of the marketplace, too. Here are some of the requirements for becoming a successful day trader.

Information and information in the forum

People who try to trade day by day without understanding the basics of the market often lose money. Technical analysis and chart reading are good skills a day trader should have. But without a deep understanding of the market and its unique risks, charts can be misleading. Do your best to understand the specific details and output of your products.

Enough Capital

Daily traders use only risk money that they can afford to lose. This protects them from financial harm and helps to eradicate feelings from their trade. A large amount of money is often needed in order to successfully use the day price movement. Access to finance is very important because day-to-day trading takes advantage of the high-interest rate on margin accounts, and volatile market fluctuations can result in large margin calls with short notice.

Strategy

The trader needs a limit over the entire market. Day traders use several strategies, including trading on stocks, arbitrage, and trading issues. They refine these strategies until they produce consistent profits and reduce losses successfully.

Type	Risk	Reward
Swing Trading	High	High
Arbitrage	Low	Medium
Trading News	Medium	Medium
Mergers/Acquisitions	Medium	High

Discipline

An effective strategy does not help without discipline. Many day traders end up losing money because they fail to make a trade that meets their needs. As the saying goes, "Plan a trade and trade through a system." Success is not possible without discipline.

To make a profit, everyday traders rely heavily on market volatility. The day trader can get an attractive stock if he goes too far during the day. That can happen for a variety of reasons, including a salary report, investor sentiment, or general economic or corporate news.

Day traders also prefer stocks with a lot of liquid because that gives them the opportunity to change their status without changing the stock price. If the price rises, retailers may replace it. If the price drops, the trader may decide to sell it briefly in order to make a profit if it falls. No matter what method a day trader uses, he usually looks at trading stocks (often).

Day Trading To Make a Living

There are two main categories of professional day traders: those who work alone and those who work for a large institution. Most of the day, traders trade the live performance of major players such as hedge funds and trading desks related to banks and financial institutions. These traders are profitable because they have access to resources such as direct lines to their partners, a trading desk, big money and rating, and expensive analytics software (among other benefits). These traders often want the simplest profit they can get from arbitrage opportunities and news events; these services allow them to use this less risky trade before individual traders respond.

Individual traders often manage other people's money or simply trade their own. Few have access to a trading desk, but they often have strong obligations to a brokerage (due to a large amount of money they spend on commissions) and access to other resources. However, the limited range of these resources prevents them from competing directly with institutional day traders. Instead, they were forced to take on additional risks. Individual traders usually trade during the day using technical analysis and fluctuating trades — combined with a certain amount — to make enough profits by moving small amounts in highly liquid stocks.

Everyday trading requires access to some of the most sophisticated financial services and market tools. Day traders usually need: 4

Access to the trading desk

This is usually reserved for traders working for large corporations or those with large sums of money. The trading or interaction desk provides these traders with instant ordering, which is especially important when sharp price movements occur. For example, when the acquisition is announced, day sellers looking at the merger may place their orders before the entire market can benefit from price differences.

Many media outlets

News offers many opportunities from the day traders spend money, so it is important to be the first to know when something important happens. The standard trading room has access to many of the leading news threads, regular coverage from news organizations, and software that constantly analyzes media to find relevant news.

Analysis software

Trading software is an expensive requirement for many day traders. Those who rely on technical indicators or swindling trading rely more on software than on the news. This software may appear as follows:

Automatic pattern recognition: This means that the trading system identifies technical indicators such as flags and channels or more complex indicators such as Elliott Wave patterns.

Genetic and neural applications: These are programs that use neural networks and genetic algorithms to create complete trading systems to make more accurate predictions of future price movements.

Merchant integration: Some of these apps interact directly with the broker, allowing instant and automatic trading. This helps to eliminate emotions in the trade and to improve killing times.

Backtesting allows traders to look at how a particular strategy might have performed in the past to accurately predict its future performance. Keep in mind that past performance is not always an indication of future results.

Taken together, these tools provide traders with the edge of the entire market. It is easy to see why many unscrupulous sellers are losing money without them. Additionally, other factors that affect a trader's income for the day the market is trading are how much money they have and how much time they are willing to invest.

Day Trading Risks

Day trading can be a daunting task for the average investor, given the risks involved. The U.S. The Securities and Exchange Commission (SEC) highlights some of the day trading risks, summarized below:

• Be prepared for huge financial losses: Because day traders often lose large amounts of money in their first trading months, and many of them never finish making a profit, they should risk the money they may be able to lose.

- Day trading is a very stressful and expensive full-time job: Day trading is very difficult, and looking at lots of tick quotes and price fluctuations to see market trends requires a lot of focus. Daily traders also incur high costs, often paying their firms large sums of money for commissions, training, and computers.

- Day traders rely heavily on borrowing: Day trading strategies use the power of borrowed money to make a profit, which is why many day traders not only lose all their money but also end up in debt.

- Do not believe simple profit claims: Beware of "hot tips" and "expert advice" from newsletters and websites that provide daily traders, and remember that educational conferences and classes about day trading may not be objective.

Should You Start Trading Day?

As mentioned above, trading day by day can be very difficult and challenging.6

First, you need to come in with some knowledge of the trading world and have a good idea of your risk tolerance, big money, and goals.

Day trading is also a time-consuming task. If you want to complete your strategy — after you have practised, anyway — and made money, you need to invest a lot of time in it. This is not something you can do from time to time whenever you get a wish. You have to be fully invested in it.

If you decide that the joy of trading is good for you, remember to start small. Focus on a few stocks rather than enter the market first and wear them thin. Going all out will cover your trading strategy and could mean a huge loss.

Lastly, stay calm and try to keep emotions out of your business. The more you do, the more you will be able to stick to your plan. Keeping your head up allows you to maintain your focus while keeping you on the path you have chosen to go down.

If you follow these simple guidelines, you are probably moving toward a more stable day-to-day business.

Is Day Trading Illegal?

Even if trading is illegal or legal, it may seem extremely dangerous. Because many day trading strategies use force on margin accounts, day traders may lose more than what they have invested and end up with huge debts.

How Can Arbitrage Be Employed As A Day Trading Strategy?

Arbitrage purchases simultaneously with the sale of the same collateral in different markets to benefit from a small difference in the price of the collateral in these markets. Because arbitrage provides a way to ensure that any asset deviation from its fair value is rectified as soon as possible, arbitrage opportunities do not usually last long.

Why Do Modern-Day Traders Succeed In Their Lives?

Day traders usually do not hold positions overnight for a number of reasons: Many traders have high demands for overnight trading, so more money is needed; stock can go down or up in the night news, causing significant trading losses; and holding the position overnight losses in the hope that part or all of the losses can be recovered may violate the trader's core philosophy of day trading.

What Are the Margin Requirements for Daily Traders?

According to the rules of the Financial Industry Regulatory Authority (FINRA), the minimum requirement for a client of a trader-designated day trader is $ 25,000, which must be credited to the customer's account prior to any day trading activities. and maintained at all times.

What Is The Power To Buy On Day Trading?

Purchasing power means the amount of money an investor has to trade in securities, and is equal to the amount of money held in the account and the genes available. According to FINRA rules, a merchant client appointed as a pattern day trader may trade up to four times his or her maintenance amount as close to the previous business day to receive shares.

Bottom Line

Although day trading has become a controversial issue, it can be an effective way to make a profit. Day traders, both institutions and individuals, play an important role in the market by keeping markets running smoothly and efficiently. Although day trading is still popular among inexperienced traders, it should be left especially to those who have the skills and resources needed to succeed.

Be a Better Investor

Managing your portfolio today can help you plan ahead for your financial future. By searching Alpha Premium, you will get access to high value stock, price ratings, and unlimited call texts. You will also find access to special authors' ratings and salary call sounds. Join over 200,000 subscribers and get unlimited access to all Premium articles. Learn more about Alpha Search and sign up for the free trial today.

Chapter One
Fundamental trading
strategies

Choosing the Very Strong Connection

When trading currencies, many traders make the mistake of formulating ideas around just one currency without considering the related strengths and weaknesses of both pairs of currencies. They trade. In the FX market, this is ignored by foreign economic conditions has the potential to significantly disrupt trade profits. It also increases the risk of loss. When you trade against a strong economy, there additional area of failure; the money you want to trade may go wrong, it leaves you stuck to money that you might have enjoyed.

Likewise, there is an additional chance that some of the money may be strengthened, which leads to less profitable trade. Therefore, finding a strong economic / weak pair is a good strategy you can use when trying increase recovery. Take for example March 22, 2005-U.S. The Federal Reserve went up its inflation risk in its statement from the Federal Open Market Committee (FOMC), which causes all major collateral to face the dollar. Once in this regard, a large amount of U.S. economic data it also strengthened the strength of the dollar. Although perhaps you could benefit from any long-term dollar trading at the time, in some pairs the value of the dollar was much higher more resilience than others. For example, after the initial bloodshed, the pound showed a recurrence in weeks after a Fed meeting, while the yen dropped for a long time.

The reason is that at the time, the British economy was experiencing steady, impressive economic growth, which, after the compulsion of the dollar, helped it get back to a certain point in the middle of a particular issue. a few weeks. A return to the British pound against the dollar can be seen in Fig 1. After a low hit of 1.8595 on March 28, the couple continued to go back to its previous FOMC level of 1.9200 in the next three weeks.

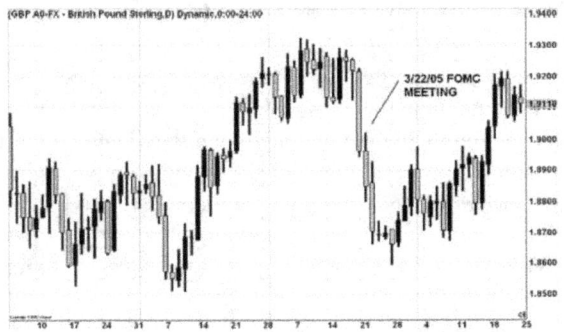

Fig 1: GBP/USD Post Fed Meeting

decline in value over too long with continuous escalating movements in USD / JPY pairs well in mid-April. This value action can be seen in Fig 2.

Fig 2: USD/JPY Post Fed Meeting

After the FOMC meeting, the dollar continued to strengthen another 300 pips over the next two weeks. Part of the reason is that the difference in this movement was that the market viewers did not have it great faith in the Japanese economy, which had been disrupted the limit of the economic downturn and not showing signs of positive economic growth. Therefore, the strength of the dollar has had a tremendous impact and has risen the amount of energy to stay with the yen is harder than ever strong pound.

Of course, interest rates and other geopolitical macro events they are also important, but if you weigh the two equally compelling trade, finding a better strong economy and weak economic integration can lead high chances of success. Exploring large crosses during this time shows another way information for different powers currency pairs can be used to maximize profits. For example, take refer to Fig 3 and Fig 4.

Fig 3: AUD/JPY Post Fed Meeting

FIG 4: EUR/JPY Post Fed Meeting

Following the FOMC meeting on March 22, both AUD / JPY and EUR / JPY were sold out, but AUD / JPY was replenished. much faster than EUR / JPY. One of the reasons why this might be what happened could be a strong economy / weak economic comparison. The Eurozone economy experienced the weakest growth in 2003, 2004, and 2005. Australia, on the other hand, is doing much better and throughout 2004 and the first half of 2005 Australia provided one of the highest interest rates in the industrialized world. As a result, as indicated In Fig 3, the pair also rose faster than EUR / JPY send FOMC. That is why when you want to trade, it is important to keep strong economy / weak economic pair in mind.

LEVERAGED CARRY TRADE

The leveraged carry trade strategy is one of the most popular trading strategies of global macro hedge funds and investment banks. It is quintessential major trade worldwide. In short, a freight trading strategy involves long journeys or buy more productive money and sell or reduce low yields money. Fierce speculators will leave the exposure of the exchange rate unvaccinated, which means the bettor is betting more productive money. money will be better than earning interest rate differences between the two currencies.

For those who circle the exchange interest rate exposure, although interest rate variations are usually small, on the scale of 1 to 5 percent, if traders enter the rate of 5 to 10 times, profits from interest rates alone can be huge. Just think about it: A The 2.5 percent interest rate difference is 25 percent with a height of 10 times. Everage can be very dangerous if not managed properly because it can increase losses. Borrowing usually happens when the amount traders see this same opportunity and accumulate in the trade, the latter to combine a pair of coins.

In foreign exchange trading, commodity trading is an easy way to apply this basic economic system in which money is constantly flowing in and out of different markets, driven by the supply chain economic law. and demand: markets that offer the highest return on investment will enter generally to attract more capital.

Countries are no different — in the world of international currency flows, countries offer very high interest rates it will usually attract more investment and create greater demand their funds. The most popular trading strategy, portable trading is easy to do well. Properly covered, it will withstand a great deal of adverse conditions taking great risk. However, commodity trading comes with some risks. the chances of losing are great if you do not understand how, why, and when trade trades work much better.

How Do Carry Trades Work?

The way carry trade works is to buy the kind of money that gives the highest interest rate while selling a currency that offers a lower interest rate. Carry trade is there profit because the investor is able to earn interest-difference spread — between two currencies. Example: Imagine that the Australian dollar offers interest rates of 4.75 percent, while the Swiss franc gives an interest rate of 0.25 percent.

To make a carrier trade, an investor buys an Australian dollar and sells it Swiss franc. By doing so, he could earn a profit of 4.50 percent (4.75 the percentage of interest earned minus 0.25 percent of the interest paid), as long as the exchange rate between the Australian dollar and the Swiss franc does not exist change. This return is based on zero on average. A five-fold ratio equals a 22.5 percent returns in dividends only interest. To illustrate, take a see the following example and Fig 5 to see what an investor can do actually do the carrier trade:

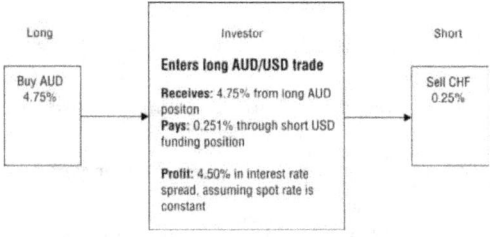

Fig 5: Leveraged Carry Trade Example

Doing Carry Trade

✓ Buy AUD and sell CHF (long AUD / CHF).

✓ Long AUD position: investor earns 4.75 percent.

✓ Short term CHF position: investor pays 0.25 percent.

Since the local rate has not changed, the profit is 4.50 percent, or 450 points. If the stock pair rises again in value due to other traders identifying this opportunity, the stockbroker will not only benefit from the harvest but also. financial gratitude.

Summary: The carrier trade operates by purchasing a currency type that offers a high interest rate while selling a currency that offers a low interest rate.

Why Do Carry Trades Work?

Cary trades have become effective due to the constant flow of capital in and abroad. Interest rates are a major factor in making some countries attractive a huge investment compared to others. If the world economy do well (high growth, high productivity, low unemployment, rising income, etc.), will be able to provide those who invest in the country a high return on investment. One way to make this point is to say it countries with better growth potential can afford this high rate interest on investments. Investors prefer high interest rates, so investors who are interested in maximizing their profits will look for investments that give them a higher rate of return. When making a decision to invest type of currency, the investor may choose the one that offers maximum return rate, or interest rate. If a few investors do this exactly the same decision, the country will receive revenue from those who want to achieve a high level of return.

What about economically poor countries? Countries with low growth and low productivity will not be able to provide investors with a high level of return on investment. In fact, there are countries with relatively weak economies that are unable to provide any return on investment, which means that interest rates are zero or very close to it. This difference between countries that offer relatively high interest rates low interest rates are what make carry trade possible.

Let's look again at the previous example of trading, but in a more detailed method:

Consider a Swiss investor earning a 0.25 percent per annum on his Swiss franc bank deposit. At the same time time, an Australian bank offers 4.75

percent a year on deposit in Australian dollars. Seeing that interest rates are very high with Bank of Australia, this investor would like to find a way to achieve this high the interest rate on his money. Now imagine that an investor could somehow trade for his deposit Swiss francs pay 0.25 per cent Australian dollar deposit

4.75 percent. He successfully managed to sell his Swiss franc deposit and purchased an Australian dollar deposit. After this transaction you are still the owner Australian dollar deposit paying interest rate of 4.75 percent per annum, 4.50 percent more was earning on his Swiss franc deposit. In fact, the investor has recently made a trade by carrying "buy" Australian dollar deposit, and "selling" Swiss franc deposit. The total impact of the millions of people making this transaction is that money travels from

Switzerland to Australia as investors take over their Switzerland francs and trade them in Australian dollars. Australia can attract a lot of money because of the high prices it offers. This is a revenue stream increases the amount of money (see Fig 6).

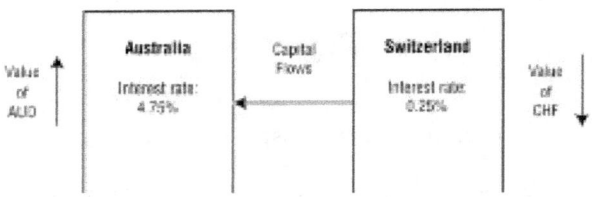

Fig 6: Effects of a Carry Trade: AUD/CHF Carry Trade Example

Summary: Carry trades are made possible by the division of

interest rates between countries. Because they prefer to earn higher interest rates, investors will look to buy and hold higher interest payers funds.

When Do Carry Trades Work Best?

Carry trades work better from time to time than others. In fact, carry trading is the most profitable when investors as a group have a positive attitude towards risk

How much risk are you willing to take?

People's emotions are appealing change over time — sometimes they may feel brave and determined taking chances, and sometimes they may be embarrassed and inclined awareness. Investors, as a group, are no different. Sometimes they are they are willing to make investments that involve a fair amount of risk, while sometimes they are very scared to lose and look to invest in safe assets. In financial jargon, which investors in general are willing to take risk, we say they have a low risk of harm or, in other words, they are in a risk seeking mode. Conversely, when investors are drawn to more savings investments and are less willing to take risks, we say they are high to hate danger. Carry trades are the most profitable when investors have a low risk of risk. This statement makes sense when you consider what a caught trade is involves. To review, the shipping trade involves purchasing a currency type that pays a high interest rate while selling low interest rate.

Ku to buy high interest rates, the investor puts himself at risk — there good uncertainty about that country economy will continue to work well and be able to pay high interest rates. Indeed, there is a good chance that something will happen to block the country from paying this high interest rate. Finally, the investor must be willing to take this opportunity. If all investors are unwilling to take this risk, then it is money it would never move from one country to another, and the opportunity to trade at carry would not exist. So, in order to work, you need to carry tasks that investors as a group have a low risk hate, or are willing to take it at risk of investing in high interest rates.

Summary: Carry trades have the potential to make the most profit over time times when investors are willing to risk investing that pays high interest rates.

When will Carry Trades be operational?

So far we have shown that commodity trading will work better if investors have it low risk hate. What happens when investors have a high hatred for risk? Carry trades are the least profitable when investors have high hatred at risk. When investors have a strong hatred for risk, they are not as determined as a team to take chances on their investment. So, they would be are less willing to invest in risky investments that offer higher interest rates. Instead, when investors hate big risk they would really like it investing in "safe" funds that pay lower interest rates.

This would be equivalent to doing the exact opposite of the carrier trade — in other words, investors are buying money at a lower interest rate and selling high interest rates Returning to our previous model, imagine that an investor suddenly feels not comfortable holding foreign currency, the Australian dollar. Now, instead of looking at the high interest rate, he is more interested in keeping his investment safe. As a result, he is exchanging his Australian dollars for Swiss francs are common. The total impact of the millions of people making this transaction is that the main money comes from Australia and goes to Switzerland as investors take their Australian dollars and trade them to get Swiss francs. As a result of this decline in the risk of serious investment, Switzerland is attracting more money for security its money supply despite a low interest rate. This is a revenue stream increases the value of the Swiss franc.

Summary: Carry trades will be a very small profit from time to time where investors are not willing to risk investing high interest rates.

The Importance of Hate Risk

Carry trades will usually be profitable when investors have low risk resentment, and unprofitable when investors have high hatred at risk. Therefore, before making a legitimate trade it is important to be careful risk area — whether investors in general are high or low risk resentment — and when it does. Increased risk aversion often has a positive effect on low interest rates: Sometimes investors' attitudes will change. immediate-investors 'willingness to engage in risky trading can change dramatically from one moment to the next. Often these major changes are caused important world events. When the deterioration of investor risk increases rapidly, the result is often the influx of high-interest "safe financial location "

For example, in the summer of 1998 the Japanese yen appreciated against the dollar by more than 20 percent over a two-month period, due to the Russian debt crisis and the Long-Term Capital Management hedge fund. bail. Similarly, shortly after the terrorist attacks on September 11, 2001 The Swiss franc has risen more than 7 percent against the dollar within 10 days time.

This sharp movement in the price of money often occurs when hate risk changes rapidly from low to high. As a result, when the hatred of danger changes in this way, the bearing trade can quickly turn into a profit for him useless. On the other hand, as it abhors investors' risk from top to bottom, treat traders for more profit. How do you know if all investors are high or low? Unfortunately, it is difficult to measure hate risk to investors number one. Another way to get a comprehensive view of risk resistance levels is to look on various bond-paid yields. If the difference grows, or spreads, among the bonds of different credit ratings, the higher the investor's hatred. Bond yields can be found in many financial journals. In addition, several major banks have developed their own risk mitigation measures that shows when investors are willing to take risks and when they are not.

Other Things to Bear in Mind When Considering a Carry Trade

Although abhorrence of danger is one of the most important things to consider beforehand doing the carrier trade, is not the only one. The following are some additional information you should know.

Appreciating Low Interest Rate

By Getting Into a Shopping Cart trading, the investor is able to earn a profit with a difference in interest rate, or spread, between the currency of high interest rate and low interest rate. However, carrier trading can turn out to be unprofitable if for some reason (as in the previous example of risk aversion) the lower interest rate is more expensive.

Without increasing resentment for investor risk, economic development conditions within a low-interest country can also determine the nature of its currency to inform. The fair trade that you carry involves lower interest rates the economy is weak and has low expectations for growth. If the economy however, the country may be able to offer investors a higher rate of return on interest rates.

If it were happening — and using the previous example, say Switzerland is growing the interest rates they offer — then investors may take advantage of these benefits high interest rates on investing in Swiss francs.

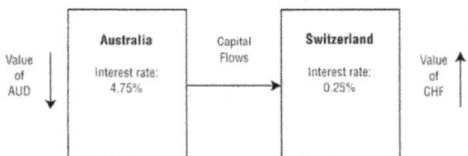

Fig 7: Effects of a Carry Trade When Investors Have High Risk Aversion: AUD/CHF Carry Trade

As shown in Fig 7, the recognition of the Swiss franc will adversely affect the profitability of Australian dollar - Swiss franc carries trade. (At least, high interest rate Swiss prices will have a negative impact on commercial gains by reducing the spread of interest rates.)

To give another example, this sequence of events is currently possible in the Japanese yen. Considering its zero interest rates, the Japanese yen has long been a suitable low interest rate money to be used in trading (known as "yen carry trades"). This situation, however, is likely to change. Increased confidence in the Japanese the economy has recently led to the expansion of the Japanese stock market. The growing demand for investors in Japanese stocks and currency has caused yen value, and this yen value has a negative impact on trading profits such as the Australian dollar (higher interest rate). Japanese yen. If investors continue to buy the yen, the "yen carry trade" will grow not very useful. This also reflects the fact that when low interest rates on the carrier trade (the type of currency traded) appreciates, negatively affecting the profitability of the bear trade.

Trade Balance

Country trade rates (the difference between imports and exports) can also affect the profitability of carry trade. We they have shown that when investors have low risk, money will flow from low interest rates to high interest rates money (see Fig 6). This, however, does not always happen. To understand why, consider the situation in the United States. The United States currently pays the lowest interest rates, yet it is attractive foreign investment, even when investors have low risk (i.e., they should invest in high-interest countries). Why did this happen? The answer is that the United States conducts much trade shortages (its exports are greater than its exports) —a deficit to be funded by other countries. In addition to the interest rates it offers, the United States is attracting revenue to support its trade deficit. The point of this example is to show that even where investors have it low risk rejection, high trade equity can cause low interest rates to be valued (as in Fig 7). And when the interest rate is lower in the stock market (the currency is traded), it is worse. affects the profitability of the bear trade.

Time Horizon

Generally, carrier trading is a long-term strategy. Previously to get into the matter of portability, the investor must be willing to commit a horoscope for at least six months. This commitment helps to make sure that trading will not be affected by the "noise" of short-term money price movements. Also, not using a lot of carrier trading power will do allow traders to hold on to their positions longer and better climate market flexibility by never giving up.

Summary: Carry trade investors should be aware of such features such as currency type information, trading balance, and horizontal pre-set trade. Any or all of these factors may result in significant side effects trading to be unprofitable.

FUNDAMENTAL TRADING STRATEGY: STAYING ON TOP OF MACROECONOMIC EVENTS

Short-term traders seem to focus only on the economic liberation of week and how it will affect their day-to-day trading activities. This works well for many retailers, but it is also important not to lose sight of the big macro events that may be imminent in the economy — or in the world at that point. The reason is that major economic events will move markets and move them significantly. Their impact exceeds the simple price change a day or two because depending on its size and width, these the occurrence has the potential to change the basic idea about the currency of months or even years at a time. Events like wars, political uncertainty, natural disasters, and international conventions they are so powerful because of their instability that they have a wide psychological and physical impact on the financial market. With these events Come on in, take a look and enjoy yourself! Therefore, to keep on top of global development, understanding the basic direction of market sentiment before and after these events, and anticipating them may be of great benefit, or at least it can help prevent major losses.

Chapter Two
How to trade like a hedge fund manager

This chapter on how to trade as a hedge fund manager is all about Steps to develop a successful trading strategy. After work And many financial managers and participants in the process Presenting the products of the managed fund, I have seen that all financial managers Work the same way. Their tactics may be different, but in the way they do it Come on in, take a look and enjoy yourself! The reason for the common threads is because professional fund managers need to be accountable. In other words, they need to understand their way of working Inside and out.

The difference between a skilled tradesman and a tradesman is one That an expert never engages in the trade of blind trade. This is important because in order for professional financial managers to have enough confidence Ask for investments in their funds, not only do they need to have a proven strategy, but they also need to know when, if the fund is successful, when It fails, and how bad things can get. As retailers or individuals, our $ 20,000 accounts are as valuable as any $20 million hedge fund. In fact, our accounts may not be the same Most importantly, because we trade our money and A $ 20 million hedge fund manager is probably trading with other people Money. Therefore, if all hedge fund managers follow a five-step process In developing their trading strategies, there is no reason why individual Traders should not do so.

The best way to improve your trading strategy is to follow a five-step process:

1. Define a trading strategy.

2. The art of entry and exit.

3. Check driving.

4. Intimacy.

5. Self-esteem.

WELL EXPLAIN TRADE STRATEGY

Every hedge fund manager, like every trader, follows a different path. Some will use only basic analysis, while others will use only Technical analysis. The first thing you need to do is find out what kind of trader you are Who you are and what kind of style you want to trade with. This chapter will not Tell you what trading style (basically compared to technology or short term Compared to long-term) will be more profitable, because there is no single style That's much better. In Millionaire Traders: How People Beat The Daily Wall Street In the Own Game (John Wiley & Sons, 2007), we interviewed 12 winners Traders from all walks of life and learn that there is no one way Trading success. Every trader is different; others would hold positions Weeks and months, while others hold them for just seconds. There are four key factors to consider when defining a Strategy, and these need to be done before you can start trading. Trading with Edit and do not update the program in an instant.

Fundamental or Technical?

The first step in defining a trading strategy is to find out who you are They want to trade based on the basics or technologies, or a combination of Both.

When fund managers develop strategic trading strategies, specify Rules are developed to code. Although not everyone Write their own trading strategies, there is a lesson we can learn from that Process, as one of the main reasons sellers fail is because they also get Emotionally. Coming up with your own rules is very important, because the following rules evoke emotions in trading. Finding out who you are You want to support your trade in news or technical indicator is just the beginning A step to define your trading strategy.

Which Currency Will You Trade?

The second step is to decide which currency pairs you want to sell, because not all created funds are equal. In FX, there are usually two types of trading strategies — the next trend or the various trades. Most Hedge funds are the next trend due to one-way bias Of the money market, but many people naturally argue again May choose to trade separately. There are no wrong or right choices, however To increase the chances of success, many hedge fund managers Will reduce the currency pairs the system will trade.

Professional traders are rarely seen using the same strategy for every single currency pair. They will probably always have currency pairs that they trade regularly and currency pairs that they do not trade at all. For example, if your trading strategy is expensive With a risk of no more than 100 pips per trade, wide currency pairs Distances such as GBP / JPY and EUR / CAD should be avoided as well It is not for sale, because even if the currency pair eventually goes the way you want it, its wide range of variables may prevent you from doing so. Other example would be to use distance trading strategies in distance trading only Currency pairs and apply trending strategies to trendy pairs.

CHF / JPY, for example, is an excellent pair of currency for a diversified and terrifying trading strategy in a trending trading strategy, because without one. The spike is low, stuck in the 300-pip range from September 2007 onwards March 2008. Therefore, the person with a different trading strategy should look Only trading currency pairs like CHF / JPY, while style traders should Avoid CHF / JPY at all costs.

When it comes to types of money, another thing to consider for majors against crosses is. Big currency pairs like EUR / USD or USD / JPY Is often more sensitive to what happens to the American dollar, however This is usually not the case with crosses, because they do not American dollar. Media advertisers can find this tip especially helpful, because Unless you trade U.S. data, crosses can actually bet better because their price action can be slightly distorted by market curiosity. U.S. Dollars

At What Time Will You Trade?

The third step to defining your trading strategy. This is to find out what time the frame you want to trade. A strategy that works on a daily chart will have very little accuracy in a 5-minute chart. For example, if by using the intraday strategy, you will find that there are many more intraday days. It is common on intraday charts and much less common on daily charts. Why is it extremely accurate when they appear on daily charts; most The rarest things can be the most valuable. Finally, other things to do when it comes to time zones.

This includes whether you hold positions overnight or longer. Weekend. For example, short-term traders may find it more profitable. Close their trades if they are not operating after a certain time or when the market moves into the Asian session. This applies to traders who react to the news because if the trade doesn't move in your market After a few hours, the momentum from the newsletter probably waned. When it comes to the weekend, sometimes something big can happen Between Friday night and Sunday afternoon. Unless you stop it You can absorb any shock or know there is no risk of major events, Closing positions before the weekend may also be something to consider.

The Art of Entry and Exit

In an interview for Millionaire Traders: How Everyday People Beat the Wall Street in His Own Game, Rob Booker made a great analogy. We Talk about whether the entry or exit of a trade is more important, and Rob likened it to flying and, more importantly, asking a pilot: Take-off or landing. As a passenger, without even asking a pilot, we will all agree that the same degree of precision must be exercised. Both takeoff and landing. This also applies to trade. Most traders spend their time trying to find the best.

Entry strategies by looking for the perfect combination of indicators for Buy and sell signals and exit strategies are often seen as an afterthought. Yet this afterthought is often constantly distinguishing profitable traders from those who are constantly looking for a better trading strategy.

I heard the traders very often They complain about how they let a winning trade become a losing trade. Hedge fund managers are a great tool when designing trading strategies. Thought agreement for both inputs and outputs. First of all, four different Ways to enter or exit a trade:

1. Single entry, single exit: Traders with single entry and single exit basically put all your positions at one price and exit them all position single price.

2. Single input, multiple output: With single input and multiple output, traders enter all their positions at a single price, but scale from the position at different prices. This tactic is often used for an escape. Or make some profit while trending for as long as possible. Path.

3. Multiple input, single output: With multiple input and single output, traders scale to a

position at different prices, but eventually all position at one price. This tactic is used by traders. Average down and average up. Lowering the mean means adding a position that moves against you in hopes of getting a better average price. Averaging means adding to a position as it moves. In your favor.

4. Multiple inputs, multiple outputs: Multiple inputs and multiple outputs exits, traders scale both to and from their positions. It's a tactic It is often used by trend traders. They come to an average position Scaling up a position to add to and capitalize on winning trades as trendy as possible.

Entry and exit strategies with automated systems are set in stone and Coded into the system. Traders should try to approach the entrances and exits. In the same way, deciding which of the four combinations to use before Goes into business. For traders who like to push the average up or down, the important question to ask is how low or how high you want to buy. If You keep adding to a losing trade, it gets smarter at some point Biting the bullet, accepting the loss and accepting your initial move The search will not happen or the trend has changed. A good rule Is to lower the average no more than three times. When it comes to stopping Should not contain art – have a set rule for placing stops and stick to it.

Test Drive

You can never buy a car without taking a test drive, so you should never trade. A strategy without back testing! For developers of hedge funds and automated trading systems, back testing is extremely important because if A trading strategy has not made money in the past, how can they believe it That the strategy will make money in the future? Many FX traders will learn Strategies from friends, trading coaches and even this book, but no one Should never blindly follow a strategy.

Make sure it is back tested and Further tested. For traders who are particularly good at programming, code your strategy using something like Trade Station, signal or Meta Trader. Make sure your results and profitable. Traders who don't know how to code should reverse the image. Scale. Open your charts, apply your indicators and 20 examples of the strategy that works. Then lower the time frame Your charts to make sure the strategy could be executed now the price you want. For example, if you are trading a strategy based on make sure there are no spikes on the 5-minute charts. Once you've found your backtested samples, it's time to test forward. One of the great things about trading currencies is the wide availability Demo and mini accounts. It is important to do a live test with a small amount money, because once real money is involved, a different set of emotions will emerge, and controlling those emotions is an important part of developing the discipline you need to trade for a large amount of money. The best thing you can do is focus on changing pips not changes in dollars.

GETTING INTIMATE

The fourth step to thinking like a hedge fund manager is getting closer With your trading strategy, because not all trading strategies are the same.

Understanding Performance

When it comes to performance, there are two main types of trading Strategies — with a high percentage of profitable trade and that Has a high profit margin. In strategies with a high percentage of profitable trading, in general The number of pips made in a winning trade is almost equal to The number of pips lost in a trade loss. An example would be a strategy When 8 out of 10 traders are winners, each successful trade makes 20 pips and each unprofitable trade loses 20 pips. Although this is not satisfactory Textbook description of a good measure of salary risk, if the number of Profitable trading is much higher than the losing trading value, strategy It is still strong. In the previous example, a total profit of 10 trades It will still be 120 pips. So, if you have a strategy like this too It starts with six or seven losers in a row, you know its time for that

Review the strategy. Strategically has a high profit margin but a low percentage of profitable trading, having a series of losers may be part of the trade site. This applies specially to emerging traders who may take less Positions with solid stops expect a major explosion. Although they May be stopped several times by 30 or 40 pips, when a rash occurs, finally the movement can be 400 or 500 pips. The important thing here is to know exactly what kind of market place you are in The strategy works well and what kind of market place your strategy fails at, because only then will you know it is time to pull the plug.

Understanding Drawing

In the money market, managing losses is very important. Many newcomers to the money market argue that FX trading is much more advanced It is more dangerous than trading any other asset. Somehow they are wrong again In some ways they are right. With only eight large coins to trade, FX Market is much easier to understand than other markets. And, since Most people only trade G-10 funds, economic data is not really possible Will be deceived and will probably not have a situation like WorldCom Or Enron.

On a daily basis, prices often do not exceed 1 to 2 percent, making it one of the least flexible assets Investing or trading. However, the availability of a very high rate does Makes trading money very risky. Some traders offer equity 400-to-1 power, making 1% move equal to 400 percent. It So it is much easier to blow up your trading account. Fortunately, profits can happen the way you want, and it is important for marketers to work consistently Manage their risk. Understanding the decline in your trading strategy helps to manage risk by giving you a reference framework for deciding when to draw Plug and where you have to stay strong. Reduction is defined as a reduction On account balance from a trade or trading chain. All professional fees Managers are able to pull the maximum of their trading strategies. Because For example, once explored a strategy that involved trading, and a high price The decline in strategy over the past 10 years has been 15 percent. Therefore number in mind, I knew that if the postponement of going forward reaches 10 percent, it does not mean that the strategy has failed. However, If the drop is up to 15 percent I should start worrying a lot; and if Up to 20 percent, so I know this might be a completely new trade Environment that was not previously calculated in the background test, and for that reason, it may be time to consider pulling the plug, I agree that I'm wrong, and I cut off the strategy.

When it comes to gravity, there are three key elements Traders need to know about their strategies. The first is the rate of downtime in a given trade; this is important because it informs you that The business behaves according to your strategy. The second is High rate of reduction; this lets you know how bad it can be. Lastly, you need to know if the pull is off or off Foundation for intrade. It is usually a pull down or a major loss of closure Trading may differ from gravity or floating loss in an open area trade.

Meditation

The final step in thinking or trading as a hedge fund manager is to think for yourself. A few years ago, after I did a FX trading workshop In Malaysia, a trader came to me for advice. He told me he was trading A strategy that has worked well in almost all areas of the market except where news is published. Interestingly, he asked me what I was thinking He should do it, and I just said, "Don't trade in the news!" Most of the time we are so busy trading that we do not see it Obviously. This is why it is important to spend some time a week or Monthly to pass or think about your trade.

At the end of it all Per week, Boris Schlossberg, my BKTraderFX running mate, and I will sit down And we have gone through all our trade. We will wonder why A certain trade worked, why it didn't work, and what we could have Done better. We will review both the successful trading and the losses we should look for Find a place to improve. In fact, with every trade we take, we will do it We wondered if this was in line with our trading strategy, and if not, it would We end up regretting making the same mistakes in our weekend reviews Sessions.

For a Malaysian retailer, little progress was needed Make may involve the avoidance of news releases, which may apply to general marketers. Some people may find that they are take advantage early or find that their performance improves by limiting Their trading at certain times of the day. Small and simple changes like These can make a long-term difference for all traders.

Chapter Three
What is the best times to trade for individual currency pairs?

The foreign exchange market operates 24 hours a day and as a result it is impossible for a trader to follow every single market organization and make a quick response every time. Time is everything currency trading. In order to design an effective and efficient investment strategy in time, it is important to be aware of the number of market functions worldwide. clock to increase the number of trading opportunities over time hours in the seller's market. Without liquidity, currency pair trading the width also depends largely on the location and characteristics of the macroeco.

Knowing what time of day it is when a currency pair has the widest range or a small trading scenario will undoubtedly help traders improve their investment experience as a result of better investment. This chapter describes the usual trading activity of large pearls in different time zones in order to see where they fluctuate greatly.

ASIAN SESSION (TOKYO): 7 P.M.–4 A.M. EST

FX trading in Asia is conducted in large regional financial institutions; during the an Asian trading session, Tokyo occupies the largest market share, following Hong Kong and Singapore. Despite the

Japanese flagging influence a central bank in the FX market, Tokyo remains one of the most important retail centers in Asia. It is the first large Asian market to open, and many

Major participants often use trading momentum there as a symbol of measuring market power and designing their trading strategies. Trading in Tokyo it can be small at times; but big banks to invest once Hedge funds are known for trying to use an Asian session to make a significant performance stop and option block levels. Fig 8 gives the level of variation currency pairs and their scope during the Asian trading session. For risk tolerant traders, USD / JPY, GBP / CHF, and GBP / JPY with good markets because its wide range provides short-term traders with profitable profit margins, 90 pips average. Foreign investment banks as well institutional investors, mostly in dollar controls, generate significant USD / JPY purchases when they enter Japanese equity and bond markets. Central Bank of Japan, more than that The $800 billion U.S. Treasury securities also play a major role in affecting the supply and demand of the USD / JPY through their open market system.

Finally, large Japanese exporters are known for their use Tokyo trading hours to repatriate, are growing currency fluctuations. GBP / CHF and GBP / JPY remain high it fluctuates as central banks and major players begin to enter positions in anticipation of the opening of the European session. For less risk traders, AUD / JPY, GBP / USD, and USD / CHF are good choices because they allow medium- and long-term traders consider the key factors when making a decision. The changing volatility of currency pairs will help protect traders and their investment strategies from being prone to improper market movements due to speculative intraday trading.

U.S. SESSION (NEW YORK): 8 A.M.–5 P.M. EST

New York is the second largest FX market, accounting for 19 percent FX market capitalization according to Triennial Central 2004 Foreign Exchange Bank Survey and Export Market Activity in April 2004, published by the Bank for International Settlements (BIS). It is the same again a financial institution that oversees the rear department of the global FX market as trading activity usually declines to a minimum from its afternoon session until the Tokyo market opens the next day.

Most of operations during a U.S. session performed between 8 a.m. once during the day, time and liquidity are high for European traders still in market. For risk tolerant traders, GBP / USD, USD / CHF, GBP / JPY, and GBP / CHF is a good choice for everyday traders from the average daily range about 120 pips. (See Fig 9.)

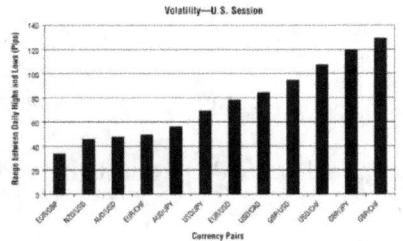

Fig 9: U.S. Session Volatility

Trading activities on these currency pairs are especially effective because these transactions directly involve the U.S. dollar. When the U.S. equity and bond markets are open within the U.S. session, foreign investors should convert their domestic currency, as such as the Japanese yen, the euro, and the Swiss franc, became less than the dollar goods to perform their duties. With market volatility, GBP / JPY and GBP / CHF have a very wide daily range. Many currencies on the FX market are quoted in the U.S. dollar. as a base and primarily traded against it before translating into something else funds. In the case of GBP / JPY, so that the British pound could be converted the Japanese yen, should be traded against the dollar first, then entered yen.

Therefore, GBP / JPY trading involves two different currency exchanges, GBP / USD and USD / JPY, and ultimately determines its volatility.

by associating two pairs of coins obtained. From GBP / USD and USD / JPY have negative affiliates, meaning their direction of movements are opposite to each other, the GBP / JPY flexibility is the same enlarged.

The USD / CHF movement can also be described in the same way but with great momentum. Trading currency pairs with high volatility can be very costly there are benefits, but it is important to remember that risk is involved it is too high. Traders should continue to review their strategies in response to market conditions because of a sudden movement in trading prices can easily stop their trading orders or make their dowry longer strategies. For risk traders, USD / JPY, EUR / USD, and USD / CAD it seems to be a good option as these pairs offer traders a decent price of the trading range to get a good profit with a small amount of risk. Their high liquid nature allows the investor to protect the profit or reduce losses quickly and effectively. The flexibility of these pairs provides an ideal environment for traders who want to pursue a long-term career. strategies.

EUROPEAN SESSION (LONDON): 2 A.M.–12 P.M. EST

London is the largest and most important center in the world, with market share of more than 30 percent according to BIS research. Most major bank sales desks located in London; most of this Large FX transactions are terminated during London hours due to the high cost and market efficiency. Large number of market participants and their high trading volume makes London a very flexible FX market of all.

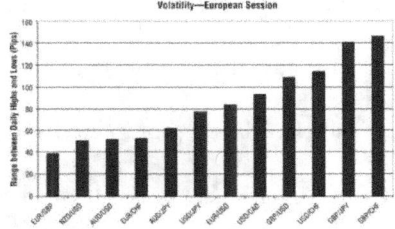

Fig 10: European Session Volatility

As shown in Fig 10, a portion of 12 large pairs exceeds 80 pipes. line, a benchmark we used to identify variable pairs in GBP / JPY and GBP / CHF reaches as high as 140 and 146 pips respectively. GBP / JPY and GBP / CHF are suitable for risk lovers. These are two pairs have a daily rate of over 140 pips and can be used to generate a large amount of profit in a short period of time. Such high flexibility these two pairs show the high value of day-to-day trading activity as major participants are about to complete their global currency exchange cycle.

London hours are directly linked to both in the U.S. Asian times; as soon as the major banks and institutional investors have completed the restructuring of their positions, they will need to start transforming European goods have become dollar-money again in anticipation the opening of the U.S. market A combination of two conversions with great players is the main reason for the very high consistency in pairs.

For risk-averse traders, there are plenty of pairs to choose from from. EUR / USD, USD / CAD, GBP / USD, and USD / CHF, on average 100 pips, which can be well chosen as its high flexibility offers plenty of opportunities to enter the market. As mentioned earlier, trade between European currencies and the dollar is growing and because key stakeholders must restructure their portfolios to unlock U.S. session For non-risk participants, NZD / USD, AUD / USD, EUR / CHF, and AUD / JPY, with a rate of about 50 pips, is a good choice as these pairs provide traders with a higher interest rate added to potential trade profits. These pairs allow investors to determine their movement divergence based on basic economic factors and to a lesser extent. often lost due to daily speculative trading.

U.S.–EUROPEAN OVERLAP: 8A.M.–12P.M. EST

FX markets are usually very active there two hours around the world large trading centers come together. (See Fig 11.)

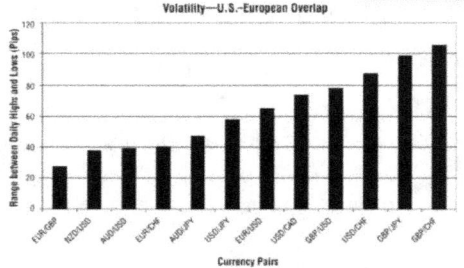

Fig 11: U.S.–European Overlap

The trading list between 8 a.m. and noon EST covers an average of 70 percent of the total value. The average trading distance of all currency pairs during the European period trading hours and 80 percent of the total total trading distance for all currency pairs during U.S. trading hours This is one percent tell the sellers of the day that if they really want a price action that is flexible too wide and you can't stay on the screen all day, trading time is U.S. meeting and Europe

EUROPEAN–ASIAN OVERLAP: 2A.M.–4A.M. EST

The trade intensity in the European–Asian overlap is far lower than in any other session because of the slow trading during the Asian morning. (See Fig 12)

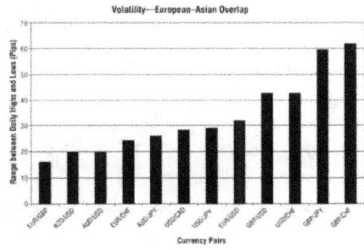

Fig 12: European–Asian Overlap

Of course, the time period surveyed is relatively smaller as well. With trading extremely thin during these hours, risk-tolerant and risk-loving traders can take a two-hour nap or spend the time positioning themselves for a breakout move at the European or U.S. open.

Chapter Four
What moves the market
(short term and long term)

What Moves the Market (Short Term)?

For basic or technical vendors, the value of economic data cannot be underestimated. Although there are many people who claim to be pure professionals, in my years in the FX market, I must understand that almost everyone will incorporate economic data into their trading strategies. A skilled tradesman who specializes in various trades, for example, may choose not to enter the market on the day the non-farm payrolls (NFP) are issued.

A technical breakout trader, on the other hand, may want to trade only on days when there is significant economic data to drive a certain high price action. Incorporating basic analysis is very important for people who trade with automated systems, because opening or closing their strategies based on incoming economic data can have a significant impact on the overall effectiveness of a trading strategy. Naturally tradesmen are often successful in economic downturns, and economic data often has a significant impact on inflation. About 90 percent of all payments are made against the U.S. dollar, which means that the greenback is the basis or counter currency for most jobs.

NOT ALL ITEMS ARE PROVIDED ECONOMICLY EQUALITY WAS CREATED

Some economic data releases can have a significant and lasting impact on the currency, while others may not matter at all. In the first issue of Day Trading the Currency Market (John Wiley & Sons, 2005), I observed that the various components of U.S. economic data how they affect the dollar (against the euro) in 2004. I chose EUR / USD because it is a highly compatible liquid currency in the world and tends to have a pure response to U.S. numbers.

Not just having positions has changed, but also the magnitude of the response has changed. For the purposes of this study, I have looked at how EUR / USD responds to it various economic releases 20 minutes after the issuance of the number again 60 minutes or one hour after the number is issued, and whether the move continued until the end of the

U.S. trading period. I think for 20 minutes knee turn time, and pipeline adjustment is based on time which is the economic number issued and the closing time is 20 minutes or after 60 minutes. This method of operation can help to bring about some wild changes within the first 20 minutes, for example, the U.S. release nonfarm payrolls are still the first leading indicator in the US dollar market; is high 2004 and 2007 lists.

The reason why the NFP is so important is that because job growth has far-reaching consequences in any country. Hard work growth often leads to strong consumer spending and strong investments policies. The growth of weak jobs could lead to weak retail sales, a slower economy, and lower interest rates. Throughout 2007, on average, EUR

/ USD will deliver 69 pips (points to FX) in the first 20 minutes following NFP free.

Every day, EUR / USD delivered an average of 98 pipelines. The magnitude of the response to non-farm payrolls, or to any U.S. economic data on the issue, declined sharply between 2004 and 2007. This was due to the decline in inflation market; in 2006, FX volatility actually dropped a record low. Liquidity to the market has also risen sharply, the volume in the FX market almost doubled in the last three years. With great liquidity, the market tends to do a better job of absorbing economic liberation. On the other side of the spectrum is gross domestic product (GDP) report, which led to an average movement of 32 pips in 2007 compared 43 pips in 2004. Every day, the response to GDP in 2007 was low there are 90 pips, which means it never entered our list of many the leading market indicators of the American dollar.

Back in 2004, average daily movement in EUR / USD after GDP release was 110 pips. One of the biggest changes we've seen in the last few years the fact that the knee reaction is very cold. In 2004, we used to see multiple spikes loosen the knees followed by a follow-up. This is usually done reaction to U.S. economic data in the first 20 minutes larger than end-of-day reaction. In 2007, however, we noticed a slight knee reaction and long-term follow-up. One of the main reasons for this difference is possible it was a fact that the Federal Reserve was lowering interest rates 2007. Therefore, traders had to better assess the effects of the economic release of the Fed's next monetary policy decision. Based on our 20-minute analysis and daily response, we created the following levels of U.S. economic data:

The leading U.S. market indicators Dollar (2007 data based)

First 20 minutes:

1. Nonfarm Payrolls

2. Interest Rates (FOMC Rate Decision)

3. Inflation (Consumer Prices)

4. Retail Sales

5. Manufacturer Prices

6. New Home Sales

7. Existing Home Sales

8. Ordinary Goods Order Orders

9. Total Home Product

Every day:

1. Nonfarm Payrolls

2. Non-Productive ISM

3. Spending personal money

4. Inflation (Consumer Prices)

5. Existing Home Sales

6. Consumer Confidence (Conference Board)

7. University of Michigan Consumer Confidence

8. Minutes of FOMC

9. Industrial Production

It is also interesting to note that the non-productive ISM report appears prominently in the daily list and is not in the 20-minute list at all. With the number of components below, there is always more to be seen when it comes to ISM reporting. Traders need to keep an eye on it both hire and price components to determine how the Federal Reserve may depend next. The ISM of the service sector is even more important, however, as part of the report hire is an excellent indicator of non-farm payroll management.

Related Economic Value Data Changes Without Time

As the world changes over time, so does the value of diversified economic emissions. Between 2004 and 2007 alone, various economic indicators have appeared in our list of top indicators. For example, in 2004 he did not exist gave a second thought to the housing market numbers, because they are real The housing market was booming and everyone expected this trend to continue forever. However, by 2007, the housing market bubble was bursting again problems had spread throughout the U.S. and in the global economy. Not only that house prices were falling and property was rising, but many homeowners were forced to refrain from repaying their mortgages. This makes the health of the housing market is crucial to the U.S. economic outlook. Everyone realized that for the US economy to recover, the housing market would need to be stabilized. Therefore, retailers are beginning to respond more strongly to existing monthly real estate numbers rather than the balance of the trading report.

Interestingly, according to the National Bureau of Economic Research (NBER) a working paper entitled "Macroeconomic Results of the The Beliefs and Conduct of International Trade

Traders, "by Yin-Wong Cheung and Menzie D. Chinn, in 1992 the trade balance was actually very high moving average US dollar market index in the first 20 minutes of free. At the time, the release of nonfarm payrolls was the third. In 1999, unemployment or nonfarm payrolls took the top spot while trading balance down to fourth, the nonfarm payrolls report continues to be the leading market release in the U.S. dollar, as well as trading. the balance has completely fallen off the radar screen for most traders. Mentally, it makes sense that the market will shift its focus to different economic data and sectors of the U.S. economy. based on economic transformation. For example, trade balance may be more important when a country has uncontrolled trade remnants, while an economy with job creation problems will see unemployment data as more important. It's all about putting yourself in the shoes of a big bank manager and thinking about what the most important issues are by pressing. FX Dealer Ranking of the Importance of Economic Data: Changes over Time

GROSS DOMESTIC PRODUCT—NO LONGER A BIG DEAL

Contrary to popular belief, the GDP report is no longer the best-selling indicator of the U.S. dollar. Another possible explanation is GDP is released less often than other data used in the study (quarterly compared to month), but GDP data is also often misunderstood and interpreted. For example, GDP growth brought by exports will be good for domestic money; however, if GDP growth is a result of asset formation, the impact on the currency may be particularly negative. In addition, many components comprising the GDP report were known prior to release.

HOW CAN YOU USE THIS TO BENEFIT?

For emerging marketers, knowledge of what data is released on the day you place a trade can help determine the size and confidence of the business. For example, in the daily EUR / USD we see the triangle form as the values combine. If the nonfarm payrolls report was expected the next day (which it was), the breakout trader would do positions probably fatter the night before the big anticipation the rash followed the release. In contrast, the third merger bar was the day of GDP release. As you can see, the scope was quiet it is relatively strong despite the fact that the eruption seems imminent. Considering the fact that the 20-minute fast movement after GDP release is not even comparable to nonfarm payrolls.

The same breakout players hoping for a bigger migration to that economy the release should include only 50 percent of the same position they would have taken if the NFP had been released. The same guidelines apply to grade traders or system traders. A nonfarm payment day can be a great time to stand by and wait for prices, while the day of GDP release still offers a strong trading-based trading system - or system. All in all, knowing which economic indicator moves the market the most is very important for all traders. Knowing 20 minutes compared to the daily range is also very important, because it tells you which pieces of economic data will cause the knee to weaken and which pieces of data will have a lasting response to the financial market. It is also important to always know what data the market considers important at any given time, because as the market moves around, so do the economic data that traders will focus on.

What Moves the Market (Long Term)?

There are two major ways to analyze financial markets: basic analysis and technical analysis. Basic analysis is based on lower economic conditions, while technical analysis uses history values in an effort to predict future movements. From technology first the analysis emerges, then there is an ongoing debate as to where it is the method is very effective. Temporary traders prefer to use technology analysis, focusing on their strategies primarily on price action, while medium-term traders often use basic analysis to determine currency type. appropriate estimates, as well as estimates of your future potential. Before using successful trading strategies, it is important to understand what drives the financial movement in the foreign exchange market. The best strategies are usually those that combine both basic and technical analysis.

Complete technical design they have failed because of major fundamental events. The same thing happens with basic; there may be sharp gyrations in the price action one day after the economic news was released, which suggested that the price action it is not structured or supported by anything other than pattern formation. Therefore, it is very important that technology traders recognize the important economy data or events scheduled to be released and, subsequently, so that key traders realize the important technical standards there the market may be focused.

FUNDAMENTAL ANALYSIS

The basic analysis focuses on the economic, social, and political forces that drive supply and demand. Those who use the basic analysis as a trading tool look at various indicators of a major economy such as growth rates, interest rates, inflation, and unemployment. Key analysts will gather all this information to evaluate current and future performance. This requires a lot of work and a thorough analysis, as there is no single set of beliefs that governs the basic analysis.

Traders who use the basics need to stay informed about news and announcements which may reflect potential economic, social, and political changes nature. All traders should be aware of the broader economic conditions before making a trade. This is very important for the day traders who try to make trading decisions based on news events because although Federal Reserve monetary policy decisions remain importantly, if the rate movement already has a full price in the market, then the real response to EUR / USD, we say, would be self-proclaimed. In retrospect, currency prices move primarily based on supply and need. That is, at the most important level, money circles because there is a need for that money. Whether the need is for fencing purposes, speculation, or conversion, the actual move they are based on the need for money. Currency rates decrease if there is an overcrowding. Provision and need should be real factors predicting future movements. However, the process of predicting supply and demand is not as simple as many might think. There are many aspects to that to contribute to the supply of surplus and demand in the form of cash, such as cash flow, commercial flow, speculative requirements, and fencing requirements.

For example, the US dollar was very strong (against the euro) from 1999 to the end of 2001, the situation is mainly driven by the U.S. Internet and the growth of equity market and the desire for foreign investors to participate to these higher benefits. This demand for U.S. goods we needed foreign investors to sell their local currency and buy U.S. dollars.

Since the end of 2001, when world insecurity was growing, the United States began interest rates and foreign investors began to sell U.S. assets high yield search elsewhere. This required foreign investors to sell The American dollar, which increases supply and reduces the value of the dollar compared to others big money. The availability of sponsorship or interest on the purchase of a currency is a major factor that can affect the trading of a currency. It became the largest dollar in the US between 2002 and 2005. The official export of U.S. goods (also known as Treasury international capital flow or TIC data) has been one of the most important economic indicators awaited by markets.

Cash Flow and Trade Flow

Cash flow and trade flows create a balance of national payments, which limits the amount of cash demand over a particular period of time. In theory, a balance of payments equal to zero is required in order for the currency to maintain its current value. Invalid balance of payments the number indicates that capital is leaving the economy at a faster rate rather than income, so money should be reduced in value. This is especially important in the current context (at the time of publication of this book) where the United States is using a stable trade deficit without sufficient foreign income to finance that deficit. The Japanese yen is another fine example. As one of the largest exporter in the world, Japan has a very large trade value. Thus, despite the zero interest rate policy that restricts cash flow to inflation, the yen has a natural tendency to trade higher based on trade flows, which is the other side of the equation. To be more specific, here is a detailed description of what big investments and the flow of trade entails

Cash Flow: Estimated Purchase Money and Sold

Revenue measures the total value of a purchase or sold as a result of large investments. Good cash flow balance means that the inflow of tangible or portfolio investment into the country skip the output. Wrong cash flow balance indicates presence a tangible investment or portfolio purchased by local investors rather than a passing one foreign investors. Let's look at these two types of cash flow – physical flow and portfolio flow.

Physical Flows

Physical flows include direct foreign investment by companies such as real estate investments, manufacturing, and location acquisition. All of this requires the foreign company to sell local currency and buy foreign currency, which leads to travel in the FX market. This is very important for the acquisition of international companies that involve more money than stocks. Visual flow is important to look at, as it represents the changes that are taking place in the real investment process. This flow is changing response to each country's financial health changes and growth opportunities. Changes to domestic laws that encourage foreign investment also apply to promote physical flow. For example, due to China's entry into the World Trade Organization (WTO), its foreign investment laws have been relaxed. Because of its cheap labor and attractive investment opportunities (over 1 billion people), companies around the world have flooded China with investment. In FX's view, in order to finance investment in China, foreign companies need to sell their local currency and buy Chinese renminbi (RMB).

The Flow of Portfolio

Flows Portfolio involves measuring revenue once and for all exit from the stock markets and fixed income markets.

Equity Markets As technology has made it easier with respect in finance transactions, investing in equity markets around the world has become very likely. Accordingly, the stock market rallying in any part of the world serves as a great opportunity for all, no matter where you are. The result has been a strong bond between nations equity markets and their currency: when the budget market grows, investment dollars usually come in to seize this opportunity. Alternatively, a slowdown in stock markets could force local investors to sell their local shares firms trade publicly to seize investment opportunities abroad.

The attraction of budget markets compared to fixed income markets has increased over the years. Since the early 1990s, the average is foreign transactions on U.S. government bonds more than U.S. shares dropped from 10 to 1 to 2 to 1. The Industrial Average had a high correlation (approximately 81 percent) with the U.S. dollar. (compared to the deutsche mark) between 1994 and 1999.

In addition, from 1991 to 1999 the Dow increased by 300 percent, while the US dollar index is valued at about 30 percent over the same period time. As a result, money traders closely follow global equity markets in an effort to predict cash flows based on short-term and medium-term stocks. However, this relationship has changed since technology the bubble burst in the United States, as foreign investors remain limited risk-averse, resulting in a low correlation between the performance of U.S. equity market and the American dollar. Still, the relationship is the same they are still there, which makes it important for all traders to look at the whole world market performance in search of intermarket opportunities.

Fixed Income Markets

Just as the stock market is associated with a volatile exchange rate, so does the stock market fluctuate. In times of the world uncertainty, a steady income investment can be very attractive, for the safety they have. As a result, the economy boasts the most important fixed income opportunities will be able to attract foreign investment — which will require the first purchase of national currency.

A good cash flow gauge is the short-term and long-term yield of international government bonds. It helps to be vigilant they spread the difference between yields and U.S. yields. 10-year Treasury note and fruit in the bonds of the Gentiles. The reason is that international investors they often invest in countries with more productive assets. If U.S. Goods have a high yield, this could encourage further investment in U.S. financial instruments, which is why it benefits US dollars. Investors can also use a temporary crop such as a two-year spread government notes to measure short-term international financial flows. Outside from the maturity of government bonds, the future of public finances can be used to measure the movement of U.S. funds, as they make prices as expected in the future.

Fed interest rate policy. The future of Euribor, or the future of Euro Interbank Given Rate, a barometer of the expected future interest rate of the euro region rates and could provide an indication of the eurozone region for future policy movements

Trade Flow: Measuring Exports Compared to Exports

The flow of trade is the basis of all international trade. Just as the investment climate of a particular economy is a key factor in it monetary equity, the flow of trade represents the balance of the country's trading balance. Countries that are exporters — meaning they export more than they import to international producers — will reap huge commercial profits. Foreigners are in a lot of opportunities in order for their prices to increase in value, as from the point of view of international trade, their money is more expensive than what is sold: overseas customers who are interested in buying a product / export service must first buy the right amount of money, thus creating a financial need for exporter.

Countries that are foreign buyers — that is, buyers more than foreign imports — have experienced what is known as trade deficit, which also has the potential to lower inflation. In order to participate in international purchases, importers must sell their money to buy that of a seller of goods or services; accordingly, to a large extent this could have a financial impact down. This idea is important because it is the main reason why so many An economist says the dollar needs to continue falling in the next few years years to stop the United States from repeatedly hitting high trade what is missing.

To illustrate this further, let us say, for example, the U.S. economy it is booming, and the stock market is growing. At that time, in the United States, a declining economy creates a lack of investment opportunities. In such a situation, the natural consequence would be for US citizens to sell their dollars and buy British pounds to take advantage of this opportunity, to promote the U.K. economy. This will lead to an outflow of funds from United Countries and inflows in the United Kingdom. From the exchange rate in theory, this could lead to a depreciation of the USD along with an increase in the GBP as the demand for USD decreases and the need for GBP increases; on the other words, GBP / USD will go up. For everyday traders, a tip to keep a broader economic picture is to find the economic data of a particular country they pile up.

Trading Tip: Chart Economic Wonders

A good tip for traders to combine the wonders of economic data against value the act of helping to define and predict future action on currency types.

Fig 13: Charting Economic Surprises

Fig 13 shows a sample of what can be done. The bar graph shows the surprise percentage of economic indicators compared to consensus estimates, while the black line tracks the price action at the time the data is released; white line is a simple line to lower the price. This chart can be applied to all major currency pairs, providing a practical guide to understanding whether the price action was in line with economic principles and to help predict future price action. This data is provided monthly at www.dailyfx.com, listed under Charting Economic Basics According to the chart in Fig 13, November 2004, there were 12. of the 15 most amazing economies and the dollar sold compared to euro in mid-December, which was the month in between economic data was released. Although this method is accurate, the analysis is easy and previous charts have shown very useful clues in future price action.

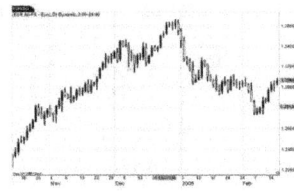

Fig 14: EUR/USD Chart

Fig 14 shows how EUR / USD fared in the following month. As you can see, the EUR / USD adjusted quickly in time in January, indicating a fundamental price difference an act that took place in December proved to be very useful in dollars, who reaped about 600 pips as the euro quickly withdrew a large portion its benefits in January. This method of analysis, called "variant perception," was founded by renowned hedge fund manager Michael Steinhardt, have produced 24 percent of the average return rate for 30 consecutive years. Although these charts rarely provide clear signals, their analysis the value may also lie in identifying and interpreting external data. Too big the good and bad of some economic statistics can be show indicators of future price action. If you go back and look at EUR / USD charts, you will see the dollar drop between October and December. This started with an increase in current account shortfalls reaching a record high in October 2004. Economic priorities are very important in the foreign exchange market than in any other market, and such charts as these can provide important indicators in price understanding. Generally, the 15 most important economic indicators are selected in each region as well then the price decline is set at the top 20 days ago price data.

TECHNICAL ANALYSIS

Prior to the mid-1980s, the FX market was largely dominated by key traders. However, with the growing popularity of technology analysis with the advent of new technologies, the impact of technology trading on FX market has grown exponentially. The discovery of a higher rate has led to a growing amount of instant or model money, which become key participants in the FX market with the ability to influence inflation. Technical analysis focuses on price movement research. Technical analysts use historical monetary data to predict future price direction. The basis of the technical analysis is that all current market information is already reflected in the value of each currency; therefore, learning the price action is the only thing you need to make informed trading decisions. Additionally, technical analysis operates under the assumption that history is common repetition

Technical analysis is the most popular tool for short to medium term traders. It works very well in the financial markets because the fluctuations in the price of the short-term currency are driven mainly by human emotions. or market ideas. A key tool in technical analysis of charts.

Charts are used to identify styles and patterns to determine profitability opportunities. The most basic concept of technical analysis is that markets have a tendency. Being able to identify trends early on the development phase is the key to technical analysis. Technical analysis combines the action of value and the momentum to build a symbolic representation of the past price action to predict future performance. Technical analysis tools such as Fibonacci retracement levels, moving averages, oscillators, candlestick charts, and Bollinger bands provide additional information about the amount of emotional overruns for buyers and sellers to direct. traders do not go to the level where greed and fear are strong. There is basically two types of markets, trendy and diversified; in the commercial sector section, attempts to identify rules that may benefit traders decide what kind of market they are currently trading in and what type they are of the trading opportunities they should be looking for.

Is Technical Analysis or Fundamental Analysis Better?

Technical analysis compared to basic is a long-term battle, and after many for years still no one is successful or defeated. Many marketers follow technical analysis because it does not require many hours of study. Technical analysts can follow multiple currencies at once. Basic analysts, on the contrary, they tend to do especially because of the large amount of data on the market.

Technical analysis works well because the financial market tends to develop strong trends. Once the technical analysis is outstanding, it can be used equally easy at any time or currency for sale. However, it is important to consider both strategies, as basic can trigger technological movements such as breakouts or trends retreat, while technical analysis can explain movement that is fundamental it cannot, especially in quiet markets, as resistant to styles the days leading up to September 11, 2001, USD / JPY had just come out of the triangle and looked ready to go up. However, as the chart shows, instead of being broken as high as the experts may have expected, the USD / JPY declined next terrorist attacks and kept hitting a low 115.81 from high 121.88 September 10.

FINANCIAL RESPONSIBILITY - ACCOUNTING AND ECONOMY

To find enthusiastic foreign exchange students who want to learn more basic analysis and financial value, this section explores various financial reporting models employed by analysts of major investment banks. There are seven major models of forecasting funds: payment balance theory (BOP), purchasing power equity (PPP), interest rate equity, currency model, real interest rate variance model, asset market model, and currency exchange model.

Payment Theory Balance

Balance payments theory says exchange rates should be in their level of balance, which is the level that produces a stable current account balance. Countries with a shortage of trade meet the run foreign currencies because they export to that nation he must sell the currency of that land in order to receive payment. Cheap money makes national sales less expensive overseas, too fuel exported and brings money to balance.

What is the Payment Balance?

The balance of the payment account is divided into two parts: the current account and the main account. The current account measures trading in such tangible and intangible assets such as cars and manufactured goods; surplus or deficit between exports and imports are called trade balances. Large account rates are flowing of money, such as investments in stocks or bonds. Payment balance Details can be found on the Bureau of Economic Analysis website (www.bea.gov).

Flow of Trade

The world trade balance reflects differences during the period between the export and export of the nation. If the country imports more than it exports the trade balance becomes worse or worse shortage. If a country exports more than what it has exported the trade balance is the same positive or residual. The trading balance reflects the redistribution of wealth between countries is also a major route through which the policies of a major global economy can affect another country. In general, it is considered wrong for a country to have lack of trade, because it has a negative impact on the national currency. For example, if U.S. trade figures show more sales than exports, more dollars from the United States and the value of the U.S.

currency come down. A good trading balance, by comparison, will affect the dollar by making it more acceptable than other currencies.

Capital Flows

In addition to commercial flows, there are also cash flows happening between countries. They record the entry and exit of the nation investment flows such as payments for all (or parts of companies), stocks, bonds, bank accounts, real estate, and industry. The capital is flowing they are influenced by a number of factors, including the financial and economic conditions of other countries. The flow of large amounts of money can be physical or portfolio investment. Often, in developing countries, the formation Cash flow tends to deviate from foreign direct investment (FDI) and bank loans. In developed countries, because of the power of equality and fixed-income markets, stocks and bonds seem to be very important there are bank loans and FDI.

Equity Markets Equity Markets have a huge impact on trading rate movement because it is a large area of high volume currency movement. Their value is great in money of countries with developed financial markets where prices are high big inflows and outflows occur, even when foreign investors are large participants. The amount of foreign investment flows in equity markets depend on the general health and growth of the market, which reflects the well-being of companies and sectors. Cash flow occurs when foreign investors move their money into something equity market. So they turned their money into domestic currency again press your need high, which makes money fun.

When I stock markets are experiencing a recession, however, foreign investors they often run away, thus turning back their household money and pushing the domestic money down.

Fixed Income Markets (Bond)

The impact of fixed income markets having money is the same as stock market and it is the result of money movement. Investor interest in a fixed income market it depends on the company details and credit ratings, as well as the general economic life and country interest rates. Movement Foreign exchange inflows and outflows into fixed income markets lead to change in demand and provision of currency, which has an impact on finances exchange rates.

Summary of Trade and Cash Flow

Determining and understanding the balance of payments in a country is probably the most important and a useful tool for those who like basic analysis. Any of the world the transaction brings two diminished entries, the trade flow balance (current account) and cash flow balance (cash account). If the balance of trade flows is a negative outflow, the country buys more from abroad than it does sells (import exceeds exports). If it is a good entry, country it sells beyond what it buys (exports surpass purchases). Balance of capital flow is best when the external income of a physical investment or portfolio in a world beyond the exit of that land. Capital flow is negative if the country buys more tangible or portfolio investments than it sells to foreign investors.

These two inputs, trade and cash flows, when put together show balance of national payments. In theory, the two inputs should be equal and mix to zero to provide for preservation quo in the national economy and inflation. Often, countries can have good or bad trade, like this and the balance of good or bad cash flow. To reduce the impact of the rest of it both on trade levels, the country should try to take care of it the balance between the two. In the United States, for example, there is a severe trade deficit, with more purchases from other countries than exports. If the trade balance is wrong, the country buys more from abroad than it sells and therefore needs to finance its deficit. This negative trade flow may be offset by the positive cash flow in the country, as outsiders buy physical investment or portfolio. Therefore, the United States wants to reduce its trade deficit and increase its capital inflows to the point where the two balances come out. Changes in this balance are very important and have serious implications for economic policy and exchange rates.

The residual effect of the difference between trade and cash flow, good or bad, will affect the way in which national currency it will move. If trade balance and capital are not right it will lead in the depreciation of the national currency, and if it accepts it will lead to financial awareness. Obviously a change in the balance of payments has a direct effect money levels. It is therefore possible for any investor to look at the economic data related to this balance and interpret the results that will occur. Financial and commercial flow data should be closely monitored. For example, if a analyst sees an increase in U.S. trade deficits declining cash flow, payment balance is missing and as a result the investor may expect a dollar depreciation

Limitations of Balance of Payments Model

The BOP model focuses on trade goods and services while ignoring international currencies.

it flows. Indeed, the flow of international currencies tends to make trade smaller financial markets in the late 1990s, however, and this often equates the current accounts of debt-laden countries like the United States. For example, in 1999, 2000, and 2001 the United States maintained its foundation lack of a large current account while the Japanese have a large current account residue. However, during this time the US dollar rose against yen although trade flows were running against the dollar. Reason was that money flowed with limited trading flows, thus undermining the BOP forecasting model for some time. Indeed, the increase in cash flow has been provided a market model of goods.

Note: It is probably a misnomer to call this method the balance of Payment theory as it only considers the current account balance, not the actual payment balance. However, it was not until the 1990s flow played a very small role in the country's economy and thus trade balance forms a large part of the balance of international payments.

Purchasing Power Parity

The theory of purchasing power is based on the assumption that foreign exchange prices should be determined by the relative bases of the same asset between the two countries. Any change in national currency rates should be weighed against a change that is contrary to the exchange rate of that country. Therefore, according to this view, when world prices rise due In the wake of inflation, the exchange rate of that country must drop to the level of equality.

PPP Goods Basket

A basket of goods and services that are priced through PPP activity a sample of all integrated goods and services gross domestic product (GDP). Includes consumer goods and services, government services, equipment, and construction activities. A lot in particular, consumer goods include food, beverages, tobacco, clothing, shoes, rent, water, gas, electricity, medical supplies and services, furniture and furnishings, furniture, transportation, petrol, transportation, leisure, entertainment and cultural services, telephone services, educational resources, goods and services for personal care and home operations, as well as repair and maintenance services.

Big Mac Index

One of the most popular examples of PPP is Big Mac Index for Economist. Big Mac PPP exchange rate that can leave hamburgers at the same cost in the United States as elsewhere, comparing these with real price signals if the currency is made at a much lower price. For example, in April 2002 the exchange rate was reached. The United States and Canada were 1.57. In the United States the Big Mac is expensive $ 2.49. In Canada, the Big Mac costs $ 3.33 in local Canadian (CAD) dollars, up to only $ 2.12 in U.S. dollars Therefore, the exchange rate with USD / CAD exceeding 15 percent apply this instruction and should be only 1.34.

OECD Purchasing Power Parity Index

An official indicator has been set issued by the Organization for Economic Co-operation and Development. Under the OECD-Eurostat PPP joint venture, OECD and Eurostat share burden of calculating PPPs. This is the latest information there currencies are less or more expensive compared to the American dollar can be found on the OECD website at www.oecd.org. The OECD publishes the table indicating prices in major industrialized countries. Each column refers to the number of specified currency units required for each countries on the list to buy the basket representing the same buyer goods and services. In each case a representative basket costs 100 units in a country whose money is mentioned.

A chart to be made then compares PPP currency type with its actual exchange rate. Chart it is updated weekly to reflect the current exchange rate. It has also been updated about twice a year to show new PPP ratings. PPP ratings are drawn from OECD studies; however, it should not taken for granted. Different calculation methods will come in a different way PPP values. According to OECD data for September 2002, the trade the ratio between the United States and Canada was 1.58 while the price The United States rate compared to Canada was 122, which is 1.22. Using this PPP model, USD / CAD is also available very important (over 25 percent, not too far from Big Mac indication only).

Limits on using PPP

Theory for PPP purchases should be appropriate can only be used for long-term basic analysis. Economic power after the PPP will eventually equal the purchasing power of the currencies. However, this can take years. Horizon time of 5 to 10 years standard. The main weakness of PPP is that it thinks the goods can be sold easily, without regard to matters such as taxes, duties, or taxes. For example, when the United States announces new commodity prices without the cost of locally produced goods rising; but that increase will not be reflected in U.S. tables. PPP.

There are other factors to consider when measuring PPP: inflation, interest rate fluctuations, economic output / reports, assets markets, trade flows, and political development. Indeed, PPP is just another of several ideas traders should use when deciding exchange rates.

Interest Rate Equality

Interest rate theory theory states that if two different types of money have four different interest rates and the difference will be reflected in the premium or discounted exchange rate forward to prevent risk. arbitrage. For example, if the U.S. interest rate is 3 percent and the Japanese interest rate is 1 percent, then the US dollar should drop The Japanese yen is 2 percent to prevent harmless speculation.

This is the future the exchange rate is reflected in the exchange rate quoted today In our example, the dollar exchange rate is said to be discounted because it buys fewer Japanese yen at a price that goes further than the local rate. The yen is said to be very expensive. Interest rates have shown little evidence of performance in recent years. High interest rates are often on the rise due to the determination of investors who are trying to slow down the developing economy by hiking prices and have nothing to do with risk-free arbitrage.

Financial Model

The monetary model states that exchange rates are determined by a country's monetary policy.

Countries that follow a stable monetary policy over time often have more favorable currencies depending on the financial model. Countries with flexible monetary policy or policies that extend beyond their monetary policy should see the value of their currency fluctuate.

How to Use a Financial Model

There are a few factors that influence exchange rates under this perspective:

1. National currency.

2. Future levels are expected for national funding.

3. The growth rate of the national currency.

All of these factors are important for understanding and recognizing money a practice that may force a change in trading levels. For example, the Japanese

The economy has been in and out of recession for more than a decade. Interest rates are close to zero, and the lack of an annual budget prevents the Japanese in applying their way out of the recession, which leaves only one tool through the use of Japanese officials who have decided to revive their economy: to print extra money. By buying stocks and bonds, the Bank of Japan increases the national currency, producing inflation, forcing change in exchange rates.

The example in Fig 15 shows the effect of a change in cash flow using a cash model. Indeed, it is in the matter of monetary policy that extends beyond that the financial model is very effective.

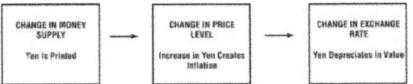

Fig 15: Monetary Model

One of the few ways the world can do it save its money on sharp reductions by pursuing strong money policy. For example, during the Asian currency crisis Hong Kong dollar was attacked by speculators. Hong Kong officials have expressed interest prices up to 300 per cent to stop the Hong Kong dollar from being issued from its peg to the American dollar. This tactic worked well as speculators they were eliminated by such high interest rates. The worst was yet the risk that Hong Kong's economy will collapse. But it is finish the pin caught and the money model worked.

Financial Model Limitations

Very few economists can no longer afford this model as it ignores trade flows and cash flows. For example, during 2002 the United Kingdom had higher interest rates, growth rates, and lower inflation rates in both the United States and the European Union, yet the pound increased in value compared to both the dollar and the euro. Indeed, the monetary model has become much more complex from the beginning of the free floating funds.

The model holds that high interest rates reflect inflation growth, which they usually do, followed by a inflation. But this does not take into account the potential revenue potential due to the high interest rate either equity market that is likely to thrive in a developing economy — the result coin that is likely to inform. In any case, the financial model is one of the few useful features tools can be used in conjunction with other models to specify the direction of the exchange rate goes there.

A Different Model of Real Interest Rate

A different theory of the real interest rate states that the movement of the exchange rate is determined by the country interest rate. Countries have it high interest rates should see their earnings in value, while countries with low interest rates should see their currencies fall number.

Fundamentals of the Model If a nation raises interest rates, international investors will find that the nation's currency yield it is very attractive and thus you bought the money of that nation. The data from this graph shows a mixed result. Australian dollar had the largest base point spread and had the highest return against it the American dollar, which seems to confirm the model as investors buy high Aussie currency. The same can be said of New Zealand the dollar, which also has a higher yield than the U.S. dollar. and gained 27 percent compared to the USD. However the model is a bit more convincing when compared to the euro, earning 20 percent compared to the dollar (more than any other dollar). money other than NZD) or the difference in its base point was the only one 100 points. The model then comes under a difficult question when comparing the British pound with the Japanese yen. The difference in yen is 100 and yet it enjoys about 12 percent compared to the dollar. Meanwhile, the British pound gained only 11 percent compared to the dollar even though it had it a significant difference in the interest rate of 275 points. This model also emphasizes that one of the most important factors in determining is the sharpness of the response rate of interest rates is as follows the expected persistence of that change. Simply put, an increase in interest rates is just that expected to last five years will have a major impact on the exchange rate if that increase was expected to last only one year.

Interest Rate Model Limitations There is a great deal of debate among international economists about whether there is a resilience and resilience an important statistically significant link between changes in the national interest rate and the amount of money. The main weakness of this model is that it does not consider the national account balance, which relies on money flowing instead. In fact, the model tends to overemphasize cash flow at the expense of many other factors: political stability, inflation, economic growth, etc. There are no such types of items, model it can be very helpful because it makes sense to conclude that you are an investor naturally it will pull straight into a high-paying investment car reward.

Property Market Model

A fundamental basis of this view is the flow of funds in other currencies Country goods such as budgets and bonds increase demand the currency of that country (and vice versa). As evidence, lawyers point to that the amount of money invested in investment products as shares and bonds are now reducing exchange rates as a result the transaction of goods and services for import and export purposes. asset market theory is actually contrary to the balance of payments the theory as it considers the national currency account instead of its monetary account. current account.

Dollar-Driven Theory

Throughout 1999, many scholars have debated this the dollar would fall against the euro in the wake of U.S. growth Lack of current account and Wall Street with the highest value. That was based the reason why non-U.S. investors they will start withdrawing their funds from U.S. stocks and bonds to economically stable markets, which it will weigh heavily on the dollar. Yet such fears have persisted ever since in the early 1980s when the current U.S. account. rises to a record high 3.5 percent of GDP. Over the past two decades, the balance of payments has been steady examining the behavior of the dollar has given way to the commodity market approach. This idea continues to hold a lot of power over the right pundits by the size of the major U.S. markets. May and June 2002 dollar dropped more than a thousand points compared to the yen at the same time stock investors have fled the U.S. stock market due to accounting scandals which plagued Wall Street. As the scandal ends at the end The 2002 dollar increased by 500 points from a low of 115.43 to close 120.00 against the yen although the current account balance is still available with great shortages all the time.

Limitations on Property Market Theory

The main limitation of the stock market theory is that it has not been tested and is new. It is often debated that over time there is no relationship between national equality market performance and its financial performance. The Dollar Index had only a 25 percent correlation.

Also, what happens to the national currency where the stock market is located side trading, trapped between bullish and bearish sentiment? It was situation in the United States most of the time in 2002, with money traders they find themselves reverting to old monetary models, such as interest rate arbitrage, as a result. The only time we will say that is the stock market the model will hold or be a short-term summary on the forecasting radar.

Currency Exchange Model

This currency conversion model is a continuation of the currency model as it considers the flow of national investment. It states that the transfer of private and public office from one nation to another is possible a major impact on exchange rates. Individual ability to change their assets from domestic and foreign currencies are known as currency exchanges. When this model is added to the currency model, proof indicates that a change in the exchange rate expectations of a country can have a definite effect on world exchange rates. Investors look at the financial model data and come to the conclusion that the change in cash flow it will happen, thus changing the exchange rate, so they invest accordingly, which turns the financial model into a fulfilled prophecy. Investors who subscribe to this idea simply jump on the bandwagon bandwagon exchange model on the way to the currency model party.

Yen Example

In the example of a money model we showed that in to buy shares and bonds in the Japanese government market it basically printed the yen (increasing revenue). Finance Model theorists may conclude that this growth could be sparked inflation (most yen chases a few products), reduces the need for yen, and ultimately caused the yen to drop across the board. A money changer can agree with this situation and look for benefits for this by shortening the yen or, if longer yen, by quickly exiting it position. By taking this step, our yen dealer is helping to drive market accurately in that way thus making the model of the financial model fait accompli.

A. Japan announces new stock market plan Economists are like that now predict Japan's revenue will increase significantly.

B.   Economists also predict inflation through introduction of this new policy. Observers expect a change in the exchange rate as a result.

C.   Economists expect interest rates to rise as inflation continues economy. Observers begin to pull the yen in anticipation of a change in exchange rates.

D.   Demand for money decreases as money flows more easily The Japanese economy and speculators dump the yen on the market.

E.   The exchange rate of the Japanese yen changes as much as the yen decreases in value in foreign currencies, especially those that are easily exchanged by investors (read: liquid yen crosses).

Currency Exchange Limits Between Large

currency trading currencies this model has not yet proven to be a convincing indicator, one of the exchange rate movements. Although this theory can be used with more confidence in less developed countries there hot money comes in and out of emerging markets with great effect,

there are still many variables that can be attributed to the currency model. For example, you are using the previous yen image. However Japan may try to provoke inflation through its securities repurchase program, however has a lot of money in the current account that will always support yen. Also, Japan has many political bombs that it should avoid locally, and if Japan makes it clear that it is trying to reduce its value, there will be significant consequences. These are just two of many features of the switch model that are unimaginable.

However, this model (like other multi-currency models) should be considered part of a diet with a perfect balance of FX predictions.

Conclusion

Day trading is not just about finding a strategy, doing it, and making money oodles. Day traders develop certain features, which allow them to use the strategy effectively in all market situations. When a person starts trading, he or she is less likely to have all these features. They may be strong in one, two, three, or even four, but they may have to work on other aspects. That's good news. It means successful traders are not born; they develop in the hard work that combines these features.

1. Discipline of the traders of the day

Discipline is an important factor that every trader needs. The market offers you unlimited trading opportunities. You can trade thousands of different stocks per second of the day, yet very few of those moments offer great trading opportunities. There are only about five seconds of real trading activity during the day. Every other moment is an opportunity to tarnish those five trading patterns, to take more of a trade than it should, to interrupt, to skip a trade, to get out of the trade prematurely, or to hold a trade for too long.

That doesn't mean your trade only takes five seconds. Five seconds of work means it only takes one second to place an entry order, and then you need to stay in your hands again. When you adjust your stops and objects, it can take another moment.

The important thing, though, is that your real trading time is small every day, even if you are an active day trader. For the rest of the day, you need to stay there, be guided, and wait for the trading signs. When a trading signal appears, you need to act without hesitation, following your trading plan.

Traders need to be disciplined when they do not have opportunities, but they should always be aware of potential dangers. After that, they need discipline to act as soon as possible when trading opportunities arise. When trading, traders need discipline to follow their trading strategies.

2. Patience

Patience is related to discipline. As discussed above, day trading (like trading of all kinds) requires a lot of waiting. If a trader enters or exits the market at the wrong time, they will often say, "My time is up." One might also say, "My patience is gone." Jumping, or getting out, trading too early or too late is a common problem among new traders.

They simply did not develop enough patience to wait for the big entrance and exit. This feature comes with discipline, and you need to be patient until you are called to action. Then, you need to have enough discipline to do it without hesitation.

Traders need patience in waiting for their turn to enter and leave — based on their strategies — but when the time calls for them, they need to act quickly. There is a continuous seesaw between long periods of patience, followed by different seconds of action, followed by patience again.

3. Adaptability

You will never see two trading days exactly the same. This ongoing difference creates a problem when one only looks at examples of strategy books. When they launch it, everything looks different from the way it did in the model. Maybe there is more flexibility, less flexibility, a stronger (or weaker) trend, or a range.

Successful marketers use their strategies in all kinds of market situations and know where to draw the line — for example, in the middle of the spectrum when using a trend tracking strategy. This need for rapid change requires mental flexibility. The trader should be able to look at the price action of each day and determine the best way to apply (or not use) their strategies, based on the conditions that exist on that day.

Traders need to be able to apply their strategies in real time, in all market conditions, and to know when to stay. Inconsistency with current market conditions will lead to a rapid decline in funding.

4. Mental Stability

You can also think of this feature as thick skin. The market will always throw you a losing trade, and you need to get back on track. If you feel frustrated every time you lose a trade, or your strategy fails to produce the result you expect, your life will be miserable. Loss of trade is permanent; The most successful day traders will have daily trading losses.

The difference between a successful and a failed trader is that most successful traders win more slowly than the losers than lose losers and often win more often than they lose. If your winnings are greater than your losses, you may only need to win 30% or 40% of your trade.

Some traders may win 60% or 70% of their trades, but their winnings may be equal, or even greater than their losses. In any case, trading losses occur. Daily gains can still be made despite those losses, but only if the losing trade does not buy you energy. If the loss of a trade causes you to lose focus, you are more likely to miss out on the next trade, which could be a winner.

Loss of lashes is also possible. Traders should stay focused and sensible in using the loss streak and not let financial loss affect their judgment - which will only make things worse. It requires mental strength to stay focused on making your trading plan and be aware when the market does not offer you the best opportunities for your strategy.

The trader has to resist a bunch of punches from the market. Loss is a real trade, but it is the way we do after a hard trade that makes all the difference. After you lose, go ahead, and continue to follow your trading plan. If you follow your plan, but keep losing, market conditions are probably not right for your strategy. If so, go for it. Sometimes being mentally tough means difficult choices not to trade.

5. Independence

At first, you will probably get help with your trade, whether it comes from reading articles or books, watching trading videos, or getting advice. However, in the end it is you who will set your trade and determine your success.

Finally, entrepreneurs need to develop a sense of independence, no longer dependent on others. Many traders choose this method because they find it very profitable. Once you have a business approach that works for you, you do not want other people's ideas. You do what works for you.

Some traders must learn to be independent. They jump from a consultant to a consultant, or a trade letter to a trading book, always feeling that something is missing. Maybe the service they registered for closure, and now they have no idea how to trade, because they rely so much on someone else. If you develop independence, taking early responsibility for your education, profits, and losses, you will not have those problems down the road.

Independence does not take over the world alone. Get help whenever you need it. Independence is just about improving the trading style that works for you (whether someone else helps you or not). It's about working to build a personal toolbox, so you can adjust your trading, instead of relying on others (who may not always be there when you need them).

If you are just starting your business journey, start developing your independence now. Take information from others, analyze it, make it your own, and use it well. That way, you won't have to rely on them anymore.

6. Forward Trading

Day traders cannot be trapped in the past. Although they use old data to help them make trading decisions, they should be able to use that information in real time. Like chess managers, traders always plan their next move, calculating what they will do based on what their opponent (market) is doing.

As discussed in the adaptation section, markets are not static. We cannot say that we will buy at a certain price in five minutes, and then ignore all the price details that happen in those five minutes. Day traders are always planning their next action, based on new information they receive every second. They consider the various possible scenarios, and then plan how they will use their trading system (e.g., inputs, stop losses, targets, trading management, position size) under those various scenarios.

Talk about what you need to do to get into the business. Self-expression will keep you focused on the action of value, and will emphasize your strategy in your mind. As trading approaches, think about what can happen while trading (not moving, moving more or less, moving faster or against you, moving less for you or against you), and how that will affect your mind and trade.

Go through what you will do in each situation so that you can move quickly in changing market conditions. That is forethought, and with practice it can almost always be instantaneous.

Forward-thinking traders know what to do, no matter what. It allows them to take decisive action, without hesitation. Have a specific set of protocols you can use for rare but inevitable events, such as losing your quote feed, for example. Thinking ahead takes practice and consumes a lot of mental energy at first, but the more you practice, the easier and faster it becomes.

Final Word on Day Trading Features

Most day traders are born with all these features. Instead, they are few in number and should work hard for others. You can learn these traits, which means that successful day trading is determined by you and not really your genes. Some of us are prone to weaknesses, but we can overcome them, which can help us to minimize the effects of our weaknesses.

Write down what qualities you need to work on and what your strengths may be. Ideally, do so based on trading experience, as trading often reveals weaknesses and strengths that we did not know we had. Personal inventory requires looking at your discipline, patience, adaptability, mental strength, independence, and foresight.

Frequently Asked Questions (FAQs)

How do you learn day trading skills?

The best way to learn how to trade the day is through experience, but you do not need to set up live trading for information. Using a demo or "paper" account allows you to duplicate trading information without real money. Brokerages offer these accounts alongside regular trading accounts, so you can become familiar with the brokerage's visual interface as you develop trading strategies.

How many day traders are successful?

The Securities and Exchange Commission warns that many day traders are losing big money in their first months of trading, and many who suffer from such losses will never recover in order to become successful day traders. However, if you have the money to recover that loss without compromising your ability to pay off your debts, or if you are patient with the paper business until you develop a successful strategy, you can increase your chances of success.

How many successful traders per day?

Two factors will determine how a trader responds to this question. First, how does the merchant describe success? Some may consider a successful day if they do not lose money, while others may consider just one day to be successful if they reach a fixed profit margin. Second, the amount a trader earns depends on the amount of money he spends. For example, if a day trader can make 1% a day, most would agree that a successful trading day, but that does not mean that the trader earns 1% of $ 25,000 or 1% of $ 250,000.

The Economic Disadvantages of Day Trading

Although day trading is a lucrative trading strategy, it can also bring many problems to the trader. Here we list the principal arguments against day trading.

The Human Factor

One of the most common arguments against day trading is the human factor. The idea behind this argument is that most humans consider luck a part of their strategy. However, relying on luck for trading is a bad idea and is even worse for day trading as the risk is higher. People tend to overestimate their abilities when things are going well. This leads to people taking more significant risks believing that nothing wrong can happen.

The Problem of Trading Platforms

The internet has broken many barriers for average users. A person can release a single without a label company or a book without a publisher. This trend has also caught the trading industry.

Nowadays, you can invest and day trade with as little as 200 USD through the many trading platforms and apps. However, these platforms are not as free as many would think. They need a constant cash flow, and that's why they incentivize any user to keep investing.

These platforms have turned trading into a game and keep users interested by giving them a win now and then. By doing this, they have turned trading into a slot machine that relies on luck to keep going.

This way of trading is dangerous as it can lead to significant losses for many users and an increase in poverty is always bad for any economy.

The Truth About Day Trading

Most day traders will lose money, while only 1% gets better returns than investing in a low-cost index fund. Inexperienced day traders may believe they are part of the 1% when things go well, but once the market turns on them, they might have a rude awakening.

Stocks Don't Always Go Up

Investing in stocks is an excellent idea in the long-term. However, it is only recommended if you can take on the downturns. Day traders usually buy and sell positions within a day, but this method makes the downturns even more dangerous.

You can start a new position on a stock because you heard or thought it would go up that day, and you wait for it to grow, and it just keeps going down before you know that stock is worth zero.

Is Day Trading Bad for the Economy or Not?

Day trading is indirectly beneficial for the economy. It allows markets to regulate their prices and brings liquidity to their trades. Successful day traders also help the economy by spending their earnings locally. However, there are direct negative consequences of day trading.

Day trading can be dangerous for inexperienced traders, as it can lead to significant debt. When people cannot pay a debt, it creates a problem for the economy, and it is worse when there is a lot of unpaid debt. Considering that only 1% of day traders succeed, you could argue that day trading can become a problem for the long-term economy.

Overall, it is a highly controversial topic, but there's nothing wrong with day trading if done correctly. Minimizing the risk for the trader means minimizing the risk for the economy too.

Conclusion

Although it is risky for the trader and the economy, day trading can be beneficial too. It allows markets to bring balance between supply and demand. It can also help the same markets to increase their liquidity.

As with every trading strategy, it will only help those that understand the market and are consistent with their work. If not done correctly, day trading can be harmful to the trader and the economy.

What Does the Day Trader Do?

A day trader is a person who buys or sells positions within one trading day. They do this to reduce market risk overnight and increase profits from a single location. However, day trading is considered a high level of trading, and many day traders are successful.

Day traders trade the stock market and work through various plans and strategies to make full use of all positions. They need full knowledge of the economy, stocks, resources, and everything related to trade. Another basic requirement for a day trader is to understand that you can make a lot of money, but there is a risk of losing everything.

Here are some important facts you need to know about daily trading:

Day trading does not invest. Investors keep their stocks long, while day traders will not hold a position for more than a day or two.

Day trading does not guarantee success. Day trading is more complex than other types of trading strategies. The reward is high, but also dangerous.

Therefore, there is no guarantee that you will succeed in doing the day's activities.

Day trading is very stressful. Everyday trading requires firmness and knowledge. Many day traders work all hours of trading and learn about the market when they are not working. This lifestyle can be stressful, and it is not a good option if you would like a peaceful lifestyle.

What Are the Economic Benefits of Day Trading?

Day trading can be rewarding if you are a smart person who knows how the market works. Let us consider some of the key issues that can be solved on a daily basis.

The Role of Trading in International Market Days

Day trading is important for the development of markets around the world. By buying and selling positions during the day, day traders secured stock exchange prices. Transformation creates a balance between need and provision for a particular position. However, it is only a short-term to medium-term solution for emerging markets.

Day trading can also help companies by reassuring consumers every day. For a trader of the day to sell a position, you first need to buy it. Day trading benefits the company because it makes some people decide to buy stocks, which increase prices.

Effective Day Traders Ready for Local Economics

The statement is true for all professionals or staff. The successful person will invest a lot of money in food, transportation, clothing and more. Therefore, this helps to create more demand for products and services, which creates more job opportunities. Increased employment means less poverty, and lower poverty means a better economy.

Day Trading Brings Money To The Market

The more people involved in the market, the more money flows. By buying stocks daily, daily traders ensure that investors and other traders can get rid of their assets quickly. It means that people will be able to withdraw their shares because of the money brought by day traders. People who invest in gold or long-term stocks benefit from day-to-day trading without realizing it.

REFERENCES

Ball, R., Kothari, S.P. "Security returns around earnings announcements." *Accounting Review* 66, No. 4 (1991), 718-738.

Barber, B. M., Lee, Y. T., Liu, Y. J., Odean, T. "Is the aggregate investor reluctant to realise losses? evidence from Taiwan." *European Financial Management* 13 (2007), 423-447.

Barber, B. M., Lee, Y. T., Liu, Y. J., Odean, T. "Just how much do individual investors lose by trading?" *Review of Financial Studies* 22, No 2 (2009), 609-632.

Barber, B.M., Odean,T. "Trading is hazardous to your wealth: the common stock investment performance of individual investors." *Journal of Finance* 55 (2000), No. 2, 773-806.

Booth Research Paper No. 09-33. available at SSRN: http://ssrn.com/abstract=1364014

Chae, J., Wang, A. "Determinants of trading profits: the liquidity provision decision." *Emerging Markets Finance and Trade* 45 (2009), 33-56.

Coval, Joshua D., Hirshleifer, D. A., Shumway, T. "Can individual investors beat the market?" HBS finance working paper No. 04-025; Harvard NOM Working Paper No. 02-45. (2005) available at SSRN: http://ssrn.com/abstract=364000 or doi:10.2139/ssrn.364000

Fama, E.F. "Efficient markets II." *Journal of Finance* 4, 5 (1991), 1575-1617.

Garvey, R., Murphy, A."Entry, exit and trading profits: a look at the trading strategies of a proprietary trading team." *Journal of Empirical Finance* 12 (2005a), 629-649.

Garvey, R.,Murphy, A."The profitability of active stock traders." *Journal of Applied Finance*, (2005b) 93-100.

Grinblatt, M., Keloharju, M."Sensation seeking, overconfidence, and trading activity." *Journal of Finance* 64, 2 (2009), 549-578.

Grinblatt, M., Keloharju, M."The investment behavior and performance of various investor types: a study of Finland's unique data set." *Journal of Financial Economics* 55 (2000), 43-67.

Grinblatt, Mark, Keloharju, M., Linnainmaa, J. T."Do smart investors outperform dumb investors?" CRSP working paper; EFA 2010 Frankfurt Meetings Paper; Chicago

Harris, J.H., Schultz, P.H."The trading profits of SOES Bandits." *Journal of Financial Economics* 50 (1998), 39-62.

http://ssrn.com/abstract=972807 (2010).

Ivkovich, Z. Weisbenner, S."Local does as local is: information content of the geography of individual investors' common stock investments." *Journal of Finance* 60 (2005), 267-306.

Ivkovich, Z., Sialm, C., Weisbenner, S."Portfolio concentration and the performance of individual investors." *Journal of Financial and Quantitative Analysis* 43 (2008), 613-655.

Korniotis, G., Kumar, A."Do older investors make better investment decisions." *Review of Economics and Statistics*, (2010) forthcoming.

Korniotis, G.,Kumar, A."Do portfolio distortions reflect superior information or psychological biases." available at SSRN: http://ssrn.com/abstract=1018668 (2009)

Kumar, A."Who gambles in the stock market?" *Journal of Finance* 64, 4 (2009), 18891933.

Linnainmaa, J.T."The anatomy of day traders." AFA 2004 San Diego Meetings. available at SSRN: http://ssrn.com/abstract=472182

Linnainmaa, J.T."The individual day trader." 2005 UCLA working paper.

Linnainmaa, J.T."Why Do (Some) Households Trade So Much?" Available at SSRN:

Odean, T."Do investors trade too much?" *American Economic Review* 89 (1999), 12791298.

Seasholes, M., Wu, G. "Predictable behavior, profits, and attention." *Journal of Empirical Finance* 14 (2007), 590-610.

www.ingramcontent.com/pod-product-compliance
Lightning Source LLC
Chambersburg PA
CBHW052315220526
45472CB00001B/127